W9-BGN-419

simply

Pasta
and Italian

p

This is a Parragon Publishing book
This edition published in 2002

Parragon Publishing
Queen Street House
4 Queen Street
Bath, BA1 1HE, UK

Copyright © Parragon 2001

All rights reserved. No part of this publication may be reproduced,
stored in a retrieval system or transmitted, in any form or by any means,
electronic, mechanical, photocopying, recording or otherwise, without
the prior permission of the copyright holder.

ISBN: 0-75258-738-2

Printed in China

Produced by The Bridgewater Book Company Ltd.

Art Director: Stephen Knowlden
Editorial Director: Fiona Biggs
Senior Editor: Mark Truman
Editorial Assistant: Tom Kitch
Photography: St John Asprey
Home Economist: Jacqueline Bellefontaine

NOTE
Tablespoons are assumed to be 15 ml.
Unless otherwise stated, milk is assumed
to be whole fat, eggs are medium and pepper
is freshly ground black pepper.

contents

introduction

There are two main culinary zones in Italy: the wine and olive zone, which lies around Umbria, Liguria, and the South; and the cattle country, where the olive tree will not flourish—Emilia-Romagna, Lombardy, and Veneto—but where milk and butter are widely produced. Tuscany, however, is the exception—it uses both butter and oil in its cooking because both cattle and olive trees thrive in the area.

Piedmont

The food here is substantial, peasant-type fare, although the expensive fragrant white truffle is found in this region. Truffles can be finely slivered or grated and added to many of the more sophisticated dishes. There is an abundance of wild mushrooms throughout the region. Garlic features strongly in the recipes and polenta, gnocchi, and rice are eaten in larger quantities than pasta, the former being offered as a first course when soup is not served. A large variety of game is also widely available.

Lombardy

Milan is home to the wonderful risotto named after the city and also the Milanese soufflé flavored strongly with lemon. Veal dishes, including vitello tonnato and osso bucco, are specialties of the region and other excellent meat dishes, particularly pot roasts, feature widely. The lakes of the area produce a wealth of fresh fish. Rice and polenta are again popular, but pasta also appears in many guises. The famous sweet yeasted cake panettone is a product of this region.

Trentino-Alto Adige

The foods are robust and basic here, where fish is plentiful. In the Trentino area particularly, pasta and simple meat dishes are popular, while in the Adige, soups and pot roasts are favored, often with added dumplings and spiced sausages.

Veneto

Polenta is served with almost everything here. The land is intensively farmed, providing mostly cereals and wine. Pasta is less in evidence, with gnocchi and rice more favored. Fish, particularly shellfish, is in abundance and especially good seafood salads are widely available. There are also excellent robust soups and risottos flavored with the seafood and sausages of the area.

Liguria

All along the Italian Riviera can be found excellent trattorias that produce amazing fish dishes flavored

with the local olive oil. Pesto sauce flavored with basil, cheese, and pine nuts comes from this area, and fresh herbs abound, widely used in many dishes, including the famous pizzas.

Emilia-Romagna

Tortellini and lasagna feature widely here, along with many other pasta dishes, as do saltimbocca and other veal dishes. Parma is famous for its ham, prosciutto di Parma, thought to be the best in the world. Balsamic vinegar is also produced here, from wine which is distilled until it is dark brown and extremely strongly flavored.

Tuscany

Tuscany has everything: an excellent coastal area providing splendid fish, hills covered in vineyards, and fertile plains where every conceivable vegetable and fruit grows. There is plenty of game in the region, providing many interesting recipes; tripe cooked in a thick tomato sauce is popular, along with many liver recipes; beans in many guises appear frequently, as well as pot roasts, steaks, and full-bodied soups, all of which are well flavored. Florence has a wide variety of specialties, while Siena boasts the famous candied fruit cake called Panforte di Siena.

Umbria/Marches

Inland Umbria is famous for its pork, and the character of the cuisine is marked by the use of the local fresh ingredients, including lamb, game, and fish from the lakes. Spit-roasting and broiling are popular, and the excellent local olive oil is used both in cooking and to pour over dishes before serving. Black truffles, olives, fruit, and herbs are plentiful and feature in many recipes. First-class sausages and cured pork come from the Marches, particularly on the Umbrian border, and pasta features all over the region.

Lazio

Here, there are many pasta dishes with delicious sauces, gnocchi in various forms, and plenty of dishes featuring lamb and veal (saltimbocca being just one), and a variety of meats, all with plenty of herbs and seasonings giving really robust flavors and delicious sauces. Vegetables feature, along with fantastic fruits; and beans appear both in soups and many other dishes.

Abruzzi and Molise

The cuisine here is deeply traditional, with local hams and cheeses from the mountain areas, interesting sausages with plenty of garlic and other seasonings, cured meats, and wonderful fish and seafood. Lamb features widely: tender, juicy, and well-flavored with herbs.

Campania

Naples is the home of pasta dishes, served with a splendid tomato sauce (with many variations). Pizza is said to have been created in Naples. Fish abounds, with fritto misto and fritto pesce being great favorites. Fish stews are robust and varied, and shellfish in particular is often served with pasta. Cutlets and steaks are excellent, served with strong sauces flavored with garlic, tomatoes, and herbs: pizzaiola steak is one of the favorites. Mozzarella cheese is produced locally and used to create the crispy Mozzarella in Carozza, again served with a garlicky tomato sauce. Sweet dishes are popular too, often with flaky pastry and ricotta cheese, and the seasonal fruit salads are laced with wine or liqueur.

Puglia (Apulia)

The ground in this region is stony, but it produces good fruit, olive groves, vegetables, and herbs, and, of course, there is a large amount of seafood from the sea. Many of the excellent pasta dishes are exclusive to the region both in shape and ingredients. Mushrooms abound and are always added to the local pizzas. Oysters and mussels are plentiful, and so is octopus. Brindisi is famous for its shellfish – both the seafood salads and risottos are truly memorable. But it is not all fish or pasta:

lamb is roasted and stewed to perfection and so is veal, always cooked together with plenty of herbs.

Basilicata

Here potent wines are produced to accompany a robust cuisine largely based on pasta, lamb, pork, game, and abundant dairy produce. The salamis and cured meats are excellent, as are the mountain hams. Lamb is flavored with the herbs and grasses on which it feeds. Wonderful thick soups—true minestrone—are produced in the mountains, and eels and fish are plentiful in the lakes. Chile peppers are grown in this region and appear in many of the recipes. The cheeses are excellent, and interesting local bread is baked in huge loaves.

Calabria

This is the toe of Italy, where orange and lemon groves flourish along with olive trees and a profusion of vegetables, especially eggplants which are cooked in a variety of ways. Chicken, rabbit, and guinea fowl are often on the menu. Pizzas feature largely, often with a fishy topping. Mushrooms grow well in the Calabrian climate and feature in many dishes from sauces and stews to salads. Pasta comes with a great variety of sauces, including baby artichokes, eggs, meat, cheese, mixed vegetables, the large sweet bell peppers of the region, and of course garlic. The fish is excellent too and fresh tuna and swordfish are available, along with many other varieties. Many desserts and cakes are flavored with aniseed, honey, and almonds and feature the plentiful figs of the region.

Sicily

This is the largest island in the Mediterranean and the cuisine is based mainly on fish and vegetables. Fish soups, stews, and salads appear in unlimited forms, including tuna, swordfish, mussels, and many more; citrus fruits are widely grown, along with almonds and pistachio nuts, and the local wines, including the dark sweet, dessert wine Marsala, are excellent. Meat is often given a long, slow cooking, or else is ground and shaped before cooking. Game is plentiful and is often cooked in sweet-sour sauces containing the local black olives. Pasta abounds again with more unusual sauces as well as the old favorites. All Sicilians have a love of desserts, cakes, and especially ice-cream. Cassata and other ice-creams from Sicily are famous all over the world.

Sardinia

The national dish of Sardinia is suckling pig or lamb cooked on an open fire or spit, and rabbit, game, and a variety of meat dishes are also very popular. There is fresh fruit of almost every kind in abundance. Fish is also top quality, with excellent sea bass, lobsters, tuna, mullet, eels, and mussels in good supply. Myrtle (mirto), a local herb, is added to everything from chicken dishes to the local liqueur; and along with the cakes and breads of Sardinia, myrtle will long remain a fond memory of the island when you have returned home.

Cooking with Pasta

Pasta has existed in one form or another since the days of the Roman Empire and remains one of the most versatile ingredients in the kitchen. It can be combined with almost anything from meat to fish, vegetables to fruit, and is even delicious served with simple herb sauces. No pantry should be without a supply of dried pasta, which, combined with a few other stock ingredients, can be turned into a mouthwatering and nutritious meal within minutes.

Most pasta is made from durum wheat flour and contains protein and carbohydrates. It is a good source of slow-release energy and has the additional advantage of being value for money. There is an enormous range of different types of pasta. Many are available both dried and fresh. Unless you have access to a good Italian delicatessen, it is probably not worth buying fresh unfilled pasta, but even supermarkets sell high-quality tortellini, capelletti, ravioli, and agnolotti.

Best of all, make fresh pasta at home. It takes a little time, but is quite easy and well worth the effort. You can mix the dough by hand or prepare it in a food processor.

Basic Pasta Dough

1 lb 4 oz/550 g durum wheat flour
4 eggs, lightly beaten
1 tbsp olive oil
salt

1. Lightly flour a work surface. Sift the flour with a pinch of salt into a mound. Make a well in the center and add the eggs and oil.

2. Using a fork or your fingertips, gradually work the mixture until the ingredients are combined. Knead vigorously for 10-15 minutes.

3. Set the dough aside to rest for 25 minutes, before rolling it out as thinly and evenly as possible.

Pasta may be colored and flavored with extra ingredients that are usually added with the beaten egg:

Black: add 1 tsp squid or cuttlefish ink.
Green: add 4 oz/115 g well-drained, cooked spinach.
Purple: work 1 large, cooked beetroot in a food processor and add with 2 oz/55 g flour.
Red: add 2 tbsp tomato purée.

Always use a large pan for cooking pasta and bring lightly salted water to a boil. Add the pasta and 1 tbsp olive oil, but do not cover or the water will boil over. Quickly bring the water back to a rolling boil and avoid overcooking. When the pasta is tender, but still firm to the bite, drain and toss with butter, olive oil or your prepared sauce and serve as soon as possible.

The cooking times given here are guidelines only:

Fresh unfilled pasta: 2–3 minutes
Fresh filled pasta: 8–10 minutes
Dried unfilled pasta: 10–12 minutes
Dried filled pasta: 15–20 minutes

Soups are an important part of Italian cuisine. They vary in consistency from light and delicate starters to hearty main meal soups. Although some may be puréed, the ingredients never lose their delicious flavor.

Antipasto means "before the main course" and what is served may be simple and inexpensive or highly elaborate. It usually comes in three categories: meat, fish, and

vegetables. There are many varieties of cold meats, including ham, invariably sliced paper-thin. All varieties of fish are enjoyed by the Italians; fresh sardines are particularly popular. Cook vegetables only until they are "al dente" and still slightly crisp so that they retain more nutrients and the colors remain bright.

soups
appetizers
light&meals
salads

exotic mushroom soup

The Calabrian mountains in southern Italy provide large amounts of exotic mushrooms. They are rich in flavor and color and make a wonderful soup.

Serves 4

2 tbsp olive oil

1 onion, chopped

1 lb mixed mushrooms, such as porcini,
   oyster, and white

1¼ cups milk

3¾ cups hot vegetable bouillon

8 slices of French stick

3 tbsp butter, melted

2 garlic cloves, minced

¾ cup finely grated Gruyère cheese

salt and pepper

1 Heat the oil in a large skillet and cook the onion for 3–4 minutes, or until soft and golden.

2 Wipe each mushroom with a damp cloth and cut any large mushrooms into smaller, bite-size pieces.

3 Add the mushrooms to the skillet, stirring quickly to coat them in the oil.

4 Add the milk to the skillet, bring to a boil, cover and leave to simmer for about 5 minutes. Gradually stir in the hot vegetable bouillon.

5 Under a preheated broiler, toast the bread on both sides until golden.

6 Mix together the butter and garlic and then spoon generously over the toast.

7 Place the toast in the bottom of a large tureen or divide it among 4 individual serving bowls and pour over the hot soup. Top with the grated Gruyère cheese and serve at once.

cook's tip

Mushrooms absorb liquid, which can lessen the flavor and affect cooking properties. Wipe with a damp cloth rather than rinsing them in water.

Supermarkets stock a wide variety of exotic mushrooms. If you prefer, use a combination of cultivated and exotic mushrooms.

2

4

6

vermicelli & vegetable soup

This wonderful combination of beans, vegetables, and vermicelli is made even richer by the addition of pesto and dried mushrooms.

Serves 4

1 small eggplant

2 large tomatoes

1 potato, peeled

1 carrot, peeled

1 leek

14½ oz canned cannelini beans

3¾ cups hot vegetable or chicken bouillon

2 tsp dried basil

½ oz/ dried porcini mushrooms, soaked for
    10 minutes in enough warm water to cover

¼ cup vermicelli

3 tbsp pesto

freshly grated Parmesan cheese, to serve
    (optional)

1 Slice the eggplant into rings about ½ inch thick, then cut each ring into 4 pieces.

2 Cut the tomatoes and potato into small dice. Cut the carrot into sticks, about 1 inch long and cut the leek into rings.

3 Place the cannelini beans and their liquid in a large pan. Add the eggplant, tomatoes, potatoes, carrot, and leek, stirring to mix.

4 Add the bouillon to the pan and bring to a boil. Reduce the heat and leave to simmer for 15 minutes.

5 Add the basil, dried mushrooms, their soaking liquid, and the vermicelli and simmer for 5 minutes, or until all of the vegetables are tender.

6 Remove the pan from the heat and stir in the pesto.

7 Serve with freshly grated Parmesan cheese, if using.

3

6

2

cook's tip

Porcini are an exotic mushroom grown in southern Italy. When dried and rehydrated they have a very intense flavor—so although they are expensive to buy, only a small amount are required to add flavor to soups or risottos.

noodle soup

This is a delicious and filling treat on cold winter evenings.

1

3

Serves 4

3 slices smoked, rindless fatty
   bacon, diced

1 large onion, chopped

1 tbsp butter

2½ cups dried peas, soaked in cold water
   for 2 hours and drained

10 cups chicken bouillon

8 oz dried egg noodles

⅝ cup heavy cream

salt and pepper

chopped fresh parsley, to garnish

Parmesan cheese croûtons (see Cook's Tip,
   right), to serve

1 Put the bacon, onion, and butter into
   a large pan and cook over a low
heat for about 6 minutes.

2 Add the peas and the chicken
   bouillon to the pan and bring to a
boil. Season lightly with salt and pepper,
cover and simmer for 1½ hours.

3 Add the egg noodles to the pan and
   simmer for an additional 15 minutes.

4 Pour in the cream and blend
   thoroughly. Transfer to a warm
tureen, then garnish with parsley and top
with Parmesan cheese croûtons (see
Cook's Tip, right). Serve immediately.

cook's tip

To make Parmesan cheese
croûtons, cut a French stick
into slices. Coat each slice
lightly with olive oil and
sprinkle with Parmesan cheese.
broil for about 30 seconds.

Other pulses, such as dried
small navy beans, borlotti,
or pinto beans, may be
substituted for the peas in
this recipe.

minestrone soup

Italian cooks have created some very heart-warming soups and this is the most famous of all.

Serves 8-10

3 garlic cloves

3 large onions

2 celery stalks

2 large carrots

2 large potatoes

3½ oz green beans

3½ oz zucchini

4 tbsp butter

¼ cup olive oil

2 oz rindless fatty bacon, finely diced

6¾ cups vegetable or chicken bouillon

1 bunch fresh basil, finely chopped

3½ oz chopped tomatoes

2 tbsp tomato paste

3½ oz Parmesan cheese peel

3 oz dried spaghetti, broken up

salt and pepper

freshly grated Parmesan cheese, to serve

1 Finely chop the garlic, onions, celery stalks, carrots, potatoes, beans, and zucchini.

2 Heat the butter and oil together in a large pan, then add the bacon and cook for 2 minutes. Add the garlic and onion and cook for 2 minutes, then stir in the celery, carrots, and potatoes and cook for an additional 2 minutes.

2

2

cook's tip

There are almost as many recipes for minestrone as there are cooks in Italy! You can add almost any vegetables you like, including soaked dried beans.

5

3 Add the beans to the pan and cook for 2 minutes. Stir in the zucchini and cook for an additional 2 minutes. Cover the pan and cook all the vegetables, stirring frequently, for 15 minutes.

4 Add the bouillon, basil, tomatoes, tomato paste, and cheese peel and season to taste. Bring to a boil, then lower the heat and simmer for 1 hour. Remove and discard the cheese peel.

5 Add the spaghetti to the pan and cook for 20 minutes.

6 Serve in large, warm soup bowls sprinkled with freshly grated Parmesan cheese.

creamed onion & artichoke soup

This refreshing chilled soup is ideal for al fresco dining.

Serves 4

1 tbsp olive oil

1 onion, chopped

1 garlic clove, minced

28 oz canned artichoke hearts, drained

2½ cups hot vegetable bouillon

⅔ cup light cream

2 tbsp fresh thyme, stalks removed

2 sun-dried tomatoes, cut into strips

cook's tip

Try adding 2 tablespoons of dry vermouth, such as Martini, to the soup in step 5.

1 Heat the oil in a large pan and cook the chopped onion and minced garlic until just softened.

2 Using a sharp knife, coarsely chop the artichoke hearts. Add the artichoke pieces to the onion and garlic mixture in the pan. Pour in the hot vegetable bouillon, stirring.

3 Bring the mixture to a boil, then reduce the heat and let simmer, covered, for about 3 minutes.

4 Place the mixture into a food processor and blend until smooth. Alternatively, push the mixture through a strainer to remove any lumps.

1

2

5 Return the soup to the pan. Stir the light cream and fresh thyme into the soup.

6 Transfer the soup to a large bowl and cover, and then let chill in the refrigerator for about 3–4 hours.

7 Transfer the chilled soup to individual soup bowls and garnish with strips of sun-dried tomato. Serve with lots of fresh, crusty bread.

5

minestrade lentiche

A *minestra* is a soup cooked with pasta; farfalline, a small bow-shaped variety, is used in this case. Served with lentils, this hearty soup is a meal in itself.

Serves 4

4 strips sliced bacon, cut into small squares

1 onion, chopped

2 garlic cloves, minced

2 celery stalks, chopped

¼ cup farfalline or spaghetti broken into
    small pieces

14½ oz canned brown lentils, drained

5 cups hot ham or vegetable bouillon

2 tbsp chopped, fresh mint

1 Place the bacon in a large skillet together with the onions, garlic, and celery. Dry-fry for 4–5 minutes, stirring, until the onion is tender and the bacon is just beginning to brown.

2 Add the farfalline or spaghetti pieces to the skillet and cook, stirring, for about 1 minute to coat the pasta well in the oil.

3 Add the lentils and the bouillon and bring to a boil. Reduce the heat and leave to simmer for 12–15 minutes, or until the pasta is tender.

4 Remove the skillet from the heat and stir in the chopped fresh mint.

5 Transfer the soup to warm soup bowls and serve immediately.

variation

Any type of pasta can be used in this recipe—try fusilli, conchiglie, or rigatoni, if you prefer.

cook's tip

If you prefer to use dried lentils, add the bouillon before the pasta and cook for 1–1¼ hours, until the lentils are tender. Add the pasta and cook for an additional 12–15 minutes.

1

2

3

pesto potato soup

Fresh pesto is a treat to the taste buds and very different in flavor from the jars of pesto available from supermarkets.

Serves 4

3 slices rindless, smoked, fatty bacon

1 lb mealy potatoes

1 lb onions

2 tbsp butter

2½ cups chicken bouillon

2½ cups milk

¾ cup dried conchigliette

⅝ cup heavy cream

chopped fresh parsley

salt and black pepper

freshly grated Parmesan cheese and
    garlic bread, to serve

PESTO SAUCE

1 cup finely chopped fresh parsley

2 garlic cloves, minced

¼ cup pine nuts, minced

2 tbsp chopped fresh basil leaves

¼ cup freshly grated Parmesan cheese

white pepper

⅝ cup olive oil

1   To make the pesto sauce, put all of the ingredients in a blender or food processor and process for 2 minutes, or blend together by hand (see Cook's Tip).

2   Finely chop the bacon, potatoes, and onions. Cook the bacon in a large pan over a medium heat for 4 minutes. Add the butter, potatoes, and onions and cook for 12 minutes, stirring constantly.

3   Add the bouillon and milk to the pan, then bring to a boil and simmer for 10 minutes. Add the pasta and simmer for an additional 12–14 minutes.

4   Blend in the cream and simmer for 5 minutes. Add the parsley and 2 tbsp pesto sauce. Transfer the soup to serving bowls and serve with Parmesan cheese and fresh garlic bread.

2

4

cook's tip

If you are making pesto by hand, it is best to use a mortar and pestle. Thoroughly grind together the parsley, garlic, pine nuts, and basil to make a paste, then mix in the cheese and pepper. Finally, gradually beat in the oil.

4

creamy tomato & pasta soup

Plum tomatoes are ideal for making soups and sauces, as they have denser, less watery flesh than round varieties.

Serves 4

4 tbsp unsalted butter

1 large onion, chopped

2½ cups vegetable bouillon

2 lb Italian plum tomatoes, skinned and coarsely chopped

pinch of baking soda

2 cups dried fusilli

1 tbsp superfine sugar

⅝ cup heavy cream

salt and pepper

fresh basil leaves, to garnish

deep-fried croutons, to serve

1 Melt the butter in a large pan, then add the onion and cook for 3 minutes. Add 1¼ cups of vegetable bouillon to the pan, with the chopped tomatoes and baking soda. Bring the soup to a boil and simmer for 20 minutes.

2 Remove the pan from the heat and set aside to cool. Purée the soup in a blender or food processor and pour through a fine strainer back into the pan.

3 Add the remaining vegetable bouillon and the fusilli to the pan, and season to taste with salt and pepper.

4 Add the sugar to the pan and bring to a boil, then lower the heat and simmer for about 15 minutes.

5 Pour the soup into a warm tureen. Swirl the heavy cream around the surface of the soup and garnish with fresh basil leaves. Serve immediately.

1

cook's tip

To make orange and tomato soup, simply use half the quantity of vegetable bouillon, topped up with the same amount of fresh orange juice and garnish the soup with orange peel. Or to make tomato and carrot soup, add half the quantity again of vegetable bouillon with the same amount of carrot juice and 1¼ cups grated carrot to the recipe, cooking the carrot with the onion.

2

3

creamy mussel soup

This quick and easy soup would make a delicious summer lunch served with fresh crusty bread.

2

3

6

Serves 4

1 lb 10 oz mussels

2 tbsp olive oil

7 tbsp unsalted butter

2 slices rindless fatty bacon, chopped

1 onion, chopped

2 garlic cloves, minced

½ cup all-purpose flour

1 lb potatoes, thinly sliced

¾ cup dried conchigliette

1¼ cups heavy cream

1 tbsp lemon juice

2 egg yolks

salt and pepper

TO GARNISH

2 tbsp finely chopped fresh parsley

lemon wedges

1 Debeard the mussels and scrub them under cold water for 5 minutes. Discard any mussels that do not close immediately when sharply tapped.

2 Bring a large pan of water to a boil, then add the mussels, oil, and some pepper and cook until the mussels open.

3 Drain the mussels, reserving the cooking liquid. Discard any mussels that are closed. Remove the mussels from their shells.

4 Melt the butter in a large pan, then add the bacon, onion, and garlic and cook for 4 minutes. Carefully stir in the flour. Measure 5 cups of the reserved cooking liquid and stir it into the pan.

5 Add the potatoes to the pan and simmer for 5 minutes. Add the conchigliette and simmer for an additional 10 minutes.

6 Add the cream and lemon juice. Season to taste with salt and pepper, then add the mussels to the pan.

7 Blend the egg yolks with 1–2 tbsp of the remaining cooking liquid, then stir into the pan and cook for 4 minutes.

8 Ladle the soup into 4 warm individual soup bowls. Garnish with the chopped fresh parsley and lemon wedges and serve immediately.

lemon spaghetti soup

This delicately flavored summer soup is surprisingly easy to make.

Serves 4

4 tbsp butter

8 shallots, thinly sliced

2 carrots, thinly sliced

2 celery stalks, thinly sliced

8 oz boned chicken breasts, finely chopped

3 lemons

5 cups chicken bouillon

8 oz dried spaghetti, broken into
    small pieces

⅔ cup heavy cream

salt and white pepper

TO GARNISH

fresh parsley sprig

3 lemon slices, halved

1

2

cook's tip

You can prepare this soup
up to the end of step 3 in
advance, so that all you need
do before serving is heat it
through before adding the
pasta and the garnish.

4

1 Melt the butter in a large pan. Add the shallots, carrots, celery, and chicken and cook over a low heat, stirring occasionally, for 8 minutes.

2 Thinly pare the lemons and blanch the lemon peel in boiling water for 3 minutes. Squeeze the juice from the lemons.

3 Add the lemon peel and juice to the pan, together with the chicken bouillon. Bring slowly to a boil over a low heat and simmer for 40 minutes.

4 Add the spaghetti to the pan and cook for 15 minutes. Season to taste with salt and white pepper and add the cream. Heat through, but do not let the soup boil or it will curdle.

5 Pour the soup into a tureen or individual bowls. Garnish with the parsley and half slices of lemon and serve immediately.

mixed seafood soup

This colorful mixed seafood soup would be superbly complemented by a dry white wine.

Serves 4

4 tbsp butter

1 lb assorted fish fillets, such as sea bass and snapper

1 lb prepared seafood, such as squid and shrimp

8 oz fresh crabmeat

1 large onion, sliced

¼ cup all-purpose flour

5 cups fish bouillon

¼ cup dried pasta shapes, such as ditalini or elbow macaroni

1 tbsp anchovy paste

grated peel and juice of 1 orange

¼ cup dry sherry

1¼ cups heavy cream

salt and black pepper

crusty brown bread, to serve

1 Melt the butter in a large pan, add the fish fillets, seafood, crabmeat, and onion and cook gently over a low heat for 6 minutes.

2 Add the flour to the mixture, stirring thoroughly to avoid any lumps.

3 Gradually add the fish bouillon, stirring constantly, until the soup comes to a boil. Reduce the heat and simmer for 30 minutes.

4 Add the pasta to the pan and cook for an additional 10 minutes.

5 Stir in the anchovy paste, orange peel, orange juice, sherry, and heavy cream. Season to taste.

cook's tip

The heads, tails, trimmings, and bones of virtually any non-oily fish can be used to make fish stock. Simmer 2 lb fish pieces in a large pan with ⅔ cup white wine, 1 chopped onion, 1 sliced carrot, 1 sliced celery stalk, 4 black peppercorns, 1 bouquet garni, and 7½ cups water for 30 minutes, then strain.

6 Heat the soup until completely warmed through. Transfer the soup to a tureen or to warm soup bowls and serve with crusty brown bread.

1

3

5

chicken & vegetable soup

This satisfying soup makes a good lunch or supper dish and you can use any vegetables that you have at hand. Children will love the tiny pasta shapes.

Serves 6

12 oz boneless chicken breasts

2 tbsp sunflower oil

1 medium onion, diced

1½ cups carrots, diced

9 oz cauliflower flowerets

3¾ cups chicken bouillon

2 tsp dried mixed herbs

4½ oz small pasta shapes

salt and pepper

Parmesan cheese (optional)

    and crusty bread, to serve

variation

Broccoli flowerets can be used to replace the cauliflower flowerets. Substitute 2 tablespoons chopped fresh mixed herbs for the dried mixed herbs.

1 Using a sharp knife, finely dice the chicken, discarding any skin.

2 Heat the oil in a large pan and quickly sauté the chicken and vegetables until they are lightly colored.

3 Stir in the bouillon and herbs. Bring to a boil and add the pasta shapes. Return to a boil, then cover and simmer for 10 minutes, stirring occasionally to prevent the pasta shapes sticking together.

4 Season with salt and pepper to taste and sprinkle with Parmesan cheese, if using. Serve with fresh crusty bread.

cook's tip

You can use any small pasta shapes for this soup—try conchigliette, ditalini, or even spaghetti broken up into small pieces. For a fun soup for children, you could add animal-shaped or alphabet pasta.

1

2

3

veal & vermicelli broth

Veal plays an important role in Italian cuisine and there are dozens of recipes for all cuts of this meat.

Serves 4

¼ cup dried peas, soaked for 2 hours
    and drained

2 lb boned neck of veal, diced

5 cups beef or brown bouillon
    (see Cook's Tip)

2¼ cups water

¼ cup barley, washed

1 large carrot, diced

1 small turnip (about 6 oz), diced

1 large leek, thinly sliced

1 red onion, finely chopped

3½ oz chopped tomatoes

1 fresh basil sprig

¾ cup dried vermicelli

salt and white pepper

cook's tip

The best brown bouillon is
made with veal bones and shin
of beef roasted with drippings
in the oven for 40 minutes.
Transfer the bones to a large
pan and add sliced leeks,
onion, celery, and carrots,
a bouquet garni, white wine
vinegar, and a thyme sprig,
cover with cold water. Simmer
over a very low heat for about
3 hours. Strain and blot the
fat from the surface with
paper towels.

1 Put the peas, veal, bouillon, and water into a large saucepan and bring to a boil over a low heat. Using a slotted spoon, skim off any scum that rises to the surface of the liquid.

2 When all of the scum has been removed, add the barley and a pinch of salt to the mixture. Simmer gently over a low heat for 25 minutes.

3 Add the carrot, turnip, leek, onion, tomatoes, and basil to the pan, and season with salt and pepper to taste. Let simmer for about 2 hours, skimming the surface, using a draining spoon, from time to time. Remove the pan from the heat and set aside for 2 hours.

4 Set the pan over a medium heat and bring to a boil. Add the vermicelli and cook for 12 minutes. Season with salt and pepper to taste and remove and discard the basil. Ladle into soup bowls and serve immediately.

1

2

3

pancetta & onion soup

This soup is best made with white onions, which have a milder flavor than the more usual brown variety. If you cannot get hold of them, try using large Spanish onions instead.

1

2

4

Serves 4

1¼ oz pancetta ham, diced

1 tbsp olive oil

4 large white onions, sliced thinly in rings

3 garlic cloves, chopped

3¾ cups hot chicken or ham bouillon

4 slices ciabatta or other Italian bread

3 tbsp butter

2¾ oz Gruyère or Cheddar

salt and pepper

1 Dry-fry the pancetta in a large pan for 3–4 minutes, or until it begins to brown. Remove the pancetta from the pan and set aside until required.

2 Add the oil to the pan and cook the onions and garlic over a high heat for 4 minutes. Reduce the heat, then cover and cook for 15 minutes, or until lightly caramelized.

3 Add the bouillon to the pan and bring to a boil. Reduce the heat and leave the mixture to simmer, covered, for about 10 minutes.

4 Toast the slices of ciabatta on both sides, under a preheated broiler, for 2–3 minutes, or until golden. Spread the ciabatta with butter and top with the Gruyère or Cheddar cheese. Cut the bread into bite-size pieces.

5 Add the reserved pancetta to the soup and season to taste with salt and pepper. Pour into 4 soup bowls and top with the toasted bread.

cook's tip

Pancetta is similar to bacon, but it is air- and salt-cured for about 6 months. Pancetta is available from most delicatessens and some large supermarkets. If you cannot obtain pancetta, use unsmoked bacon instead.

parma ravioli soup

This soup is the traditional Minestra served at Easter and Christmas in the province of Parma.

Serves 4

10 oz Basic Pasta Dough (see page 7)

5 cups veal bouillon

freshly grated Parmesan cheese, to serve

FILLING

1 cup freshly grated Parmesan cheese

1⅔ cup fine white bread crumbs

2 eggs

½ cup Espagnole Sauce (see Cook's Tip, on right)

1 small onion, finely chopped

1 tsp freshly grated nutmeg

1 Make the Basic Pasta Dough (see page 7). Carefully roll out 2 sheets of the pasta dough and cover with a damp dish towel while you make the filling for the ravioli.

2 To make the filling, mix together the freshly grated Parmesan cheese, fine white bread crumbs, eggs, Espagnole Sauce (see Cook's Tip, right), finely chopped onion, and the freshly grated nutmeg in a large mixing bowl.

3 Place spoonfuls of the filling at regular intervals on 1 sheet of pasta dough. Cover with the second sheet of pasta dough and cut into squares, then seal the edges.

4 Bring the veal bouillon to a boil in a large pan. Add the ravioli to the pan and cook for about 15 minutes.

5 Transfer the soup and ravioli to warm serving bowls and serve at once, generously sprinkled with freshly grated Parmesan cheese.

cook's tip

For Espagnole Sauce, melt 2 tbsp butter and stir in ¼ cup all-purpose flour. Cook over a low heat, stirring, until lightly colored. Add 1 tsp tomato paste, then stir in 1⅛ cups hot veal bouillon, 1 tbsp Madeira wine, and 1½ tsp white wine vinegar. Dice 1 oz each bacon, carrot, and onion and ½ oz each celery, leek, and fennel. Cook with a thyme sprig and a bay leaf in oil until soft. Drain, add to the sauce, and simmer for 4 hours. Strain the sauce before using.

2

3

3

mixed bell peppers with thyme

These bell peppers can be used as an antipasto, as a side dish, or as a relish to accompany meat and fish.

Serves 4

2 each, red, yellow, and orange bell peppers

4 tomatoes, halved

1 tbsp olive oil

3 garlic cloves, chopped

1 onion, sliced in rings

2 tbsp fresh thyme

salt and pepper

1 Halve and seed the bell peppers. Place them, cut-side down, on a cookie sheet and cook under a preheated broiler for 10 minutes.

2 Add the tomatoes to the cookie sheet and broil for 5 minutes, or until the skins of the bell peppers and tomatoes are charred.

3 Put the bell peppers into a plastic bag for 10 minutes to sweat, which will make the skin easier to peel. Remove the tomato skins and then coarsely chop the flesh.

4 Peel the skins from the bell peppers and slice the flesh into strips.

5 Heat the oil in a large skillet and cook the garlic and onion for 3–4 minutes, or until softened.

6 Add the bell peppers and tomatoes to the skillet and cook for 5 minutes. Stir in the fresh thyme and season to taste with salt and pepper.

7 Transfer to serving bowls and serve warm or chilled.

cook's tip

Preserve the bell peppers in the refrigerator by placing them in a sterilized jar and pouring olive oil over the top to seal. Alternatively, heat ¼ cup white wine vinegar with a bay leaf and 4 juniper berries and bring to a boiling point. Pour over the bell peppers and set aside until completely cold. Pack into sterilized jars—they will keep for up to 1 month.

4

1

6

sicilian caramelized onions

This is a typical Sicilian dish, combining honey and vinegar to give a delicate sweet and sour flavor. Serve hot as an accompaniment or cold with cured meats.

1

3

4

Serves 4

12 oz baby or pickling onions

2 tbsp olive oil

2 fresh bay leaves, torn into strips

thinly pared peel of 1 lemon

1 tbsp soft brown sugar

1 tbsp honey

4 tbsp red wine vinegar

1 Soak the onions in a bowl of boiling water—this will make them easier to peel. Using a sharp knife, peel and halve the onions.

2 Heat the oil in a large skillet. Add the bay leaves and onions to the skillet and cook for 5–6 minutes over a medium-high heat, or until well browned all over.

3 Cut the lemon peel into short, thin sticks. Add to the skillet with the sugar and honey. Cook for 2–3 minutes, stirring occasionally, until the onions are lightly caramelized.

4 Add the red wine vinegar to the skillet, being careful because it will spit. Cook for about 5 minutes, stirring, or until the onions are tender and the liquid has all but disappeared.

5 Transfer the onions to a serving dish and serve at once.

cook's tip

To make the onions easier to peel, place them in a large pan and pour over boiling water, then let stand for 10 minutes. Drain the onions thoroughly, and when they are cold enough to handle, peel them.

cook's tip

Adjust the piquancy of this dish to your liking by adding more sugar for a sweeter, more caramelized taste or extra red wine vinegar for a sharper, tarter flavor.

rice & cheese balls

The Italian name for this dish translates as "telephone wires," which refers to the strings of melted mozzarella cheese—the surprise contained within the risotto balls.

1

2

5

Serves 4

2 tbsp olive oil

1 medium onion, finely chopped

1 garlic clove, chopped

½ red bell pepper, diced

¾ cup risotto rice, washed

1 tsp dried oregano

1¼ cup hot vegetable or chicken bouillon

½ scant cup dry white wine

2¾ oz mozzarella cheese

oil, for deep-frying

fresh basil sprig, to garnish

1 Heat the oil in a skillet and cook the onion and garlic for 3–4 minutes, or until just softened.

2 Add the bell pepper, rice, and oregano to the skillet. Cook for 2–3 minutes, stirring to coat the rice in the oil.

3 Mix the bouillon together with the wine and add to the pan a ladleful at a time, waiting for the liquid to be absorbed by the rice before you add the next ladleful of liquid.

4 Once all of the liquid has been absorbed and the rice is tender (it should take about 15 minutes in total), remove the skillet from the heat and let stand until cool enough to handle.

5 Cut the cheese into 12 pieces. Taking about a tablespoon of risotto, shape the mixture around the cheese pieces to make 12 balls.

6 Heat the oil until a piece of bread browns in 30 seconds. Cook the risotto balls in batches of 4 for 2 minutes, or until golden.

7 Remove the risotto balls with a draining spoon and drain thoroughly on absorbent paper towels. Garnish with a sprig of basil and serve hot.

cook's tip

Although mozzarella is the traditional cheese for this recipe and creates the stringy "telephone wire" effect, other cheeses may be used if you prefer.

roman artichokes

This is a traditional Roman dish. The artichokes are stewed in a mixture of olive oil with fresh herbs.

Serves 4

4 small globe artichokes

olive oil

4 garlic cloves, peeled

2 bay leaves

finely grated peel and juice of 1 lemon

2 tbsp fresh marjoram

lemon wedges, to serve

1 Using a sharp knife, carefully peel away the tough outer leaves surrounding the artichokes. Trim the stems to about 1 inch.

2 Using a knife, cut each artichoke in half and scoop out the heart.

3 Place the artichokes in a large heavy-bottomed pan. Pour over enough olive oil to half cover the artichokes in the pan.

4 Add the garlic cloves, bay leaves, and half of the grated lemon peel.

5 Start to heat the artichokes gently, then cover the pan and continue to cook over a low heat for about 40 minutes. The artichokes should be stewed in the oil, not fried.

6 Once the artichokes are tender, remove them with a draining spoon and drain thoroughly. Remove the bay leaves.

7 Transfer the artichokes to warm serving plates. Serve the artichokes sprinkled with the remaining grated lemon peel, fresh marjoram, and a little lemon juice.

cook's tip

To prevent the artichokes from oxidizing and turning brown before cooking, brush them with lemon juice. In addition, use the oil used for cooking the artichokes for salad dressings—it will impart a lovely lemon and herb flavor.

2

3

6

eggplant layer

These layers of eggplant, tomato sauce, and mozzarella combine with Parmesan cheese to create a wonderfully tasty appetizer.

Serves 4

3–4 tbsp olive oil

2 garlic cloves, minced

2 large eggplants

3½ oz mozzarella cheese, sliced thinly

7 oz strained tomatoes

1/2 cup grated Parmesan cheese, grated

1 Heat 2 tablespoons of the olive oil in a large skillet. Add the garlic to the skillet and sauté for 30 seconds.

2 Slice the eggplant lengthwise. Add the slices to the pan and cook in the oil for 3–4 minutes on each side, or until tender. (You will probably have to cook them in batches, so add the remaining oil as necessary.)

3 Remove the eggplant with a draining spoon and drain well on absorbent paper towels.

4 Place a layer of eggplant slices in a shallow ovenproof dish. Cover the eggplant with a layer of mozzarella and then pour over a third of the strained tomatoes. Continue layering in the same order, finishing with a layer of strained tomatoes on top.

2

5 Generously sprinkle the grated Parmesan cheese over the top and bake in a preheated oven at 400°F for 25–30 minutes.

6 Transfer to serving plates and serve warm or chilled.

cook's tip

A simple tomato sauce can be bought from most supermarkets. Alternatively, you can purée and strain a can of tomatoes and season with salt and pepper.

2

4

stuffed omelet morsels

These omelet strips are delicious smothered in tomato sauce.

1

2

5

Serves 4

2 tbsp butter

1 onion, finely chopped

2 garlic cloves, chopped

4 eggs, beaten

⅔ cup milk

2¾ oz Gruyère cheese, diced

14 oz canned tomatoes, chopped

1 tbsp rosemary, stalks removed

⅔ cup vegetable bouillon

freshly grated Parmesan cheese, for
   sprinkling

crusty bread, to serve

1 Melt the butter in a large skillet. Add the onion and garlic and cook for 4–5 minutes, or until softened.

2 Beat together the eggs and milk and add the mixture to the skillet.

3 Using a spatula, gently raise the cooked edges of the omelet and tip any uncooked egg around the edge of the skillet.

4 Scatter over the cheese. Cook for 5 minutes, turning once, until golden on both sides. Remove from the pan and roll up.

5 Add the tomatoes, rosemary, and vegetable bouillon to the skillet, stirring, and bring to a boil.

6 Let the tomato sauce simmer for about 10 minutes, or until reduced and thickened.

7 Slice the omelet into strips and add to the tomato sauce in the skillet. Cook for 3–4 minutes, or until very hot.

8 Sprinkle the freshly grated Parmesan cheese over the omelet strips in tomato sauce and serve with fresh crusty bread.

cook's tip

Try adding 3½ oz diced pancetta or unsmoked bacon in step 1 and cooking the meat with the onions.

bean & onion casserole

This quick and easy casserole can be eaten as a healthy supper dish or as a side dish to accompany sausages or grilled fish.

Serves 4

14 oz canned cannellini beans

14 oz canned borlotti beans

2 tbsp olive oil

1 celery stalk

2 garlic cloves, chopped

6 oz baby onions, halved

1 lb tomatoes

2¾ oz arugula

cook's tip

Another way to peel tomatoes is to cut a cross in the base, then push it on to a fork and hold it over a gas flame, turning it slowly so that the skin heats evenly all over. The skin will start to bubble and split, and should then slide off easily.

variation

For a spicier tasting dish, add 1-2 teaspoons of hot pepper sauce with the beans in step 4.

1 Drain both cans of beans and reserve 6 tbsp of the liquid.

2 Heat the oil in a large pan. Add the celery, garlic, and onions and sauté for 5 minutes, or until the onions are golden.

3 Cut a cross in the base of each tomato and plunge them into a bowl of boiling water for 30 seconds until the skins split. Remove them with a draining spoon and let stand until cool enough to handle. Peel off the skin and chop the flesh. Add the tomato flesh and the reserved bean liquid to the pan and cook for 5 minutes.

4 Add the beans to the pan and cook for an additional 3–4 minutes, or until the beans are hot.

5 Stir in the arugula and allow to wilt slightly before serving.

1

2

3

cream & sage tagliarini

This simple, creamy pasta sauce is a classic Italian recipe.

1

2

3

Serves 4

2 tbsp butter

8 oz Gorgonzola cheese, roughly crumbled

¼ cup heavy cream

2 tbsp dry white wine

1 tsp cornstarch

4 fresh sage sprigs, finely chopped

14 oz dried tagliarini

2 tbsp olive oil

salt and white pepper

1 Melt the butter in a heavy-bottomed pan. Stir in 6 oz of the Gorgonzola cheese and melt, over a low heat, for about 2 minutes.

2 Add the cream, wine, and cornstarch and beat with a whisk until fully incorporated.

3 Stir in the sage and season to taste with salt and white pepper. Bring to a boil over a low heat, whisking constantly, until the sauce thickens. Remove from the heat and set aside while you cook the pasta.

4 Bring a large pan of lightly salted water to a boil. Add the tagliarini and 1 tbsp of the olive oil. Cook the pasta for 12–14 minutes, or until just tender, then drain thoroughly and toss in the remaining olive oil. Transfer the pasta to a serving dish and keep warm.

5 Return the pan containing the sauce to a low heat to reheat the sauce, whisking constantly. Spoon the Gorgonzola sauce over the tagliarini, then generously sprinkle over the remaining cheese, and serve immediately.

cook's tip

Gorgonzola is one of the world's oldest veined cheeses and, arguably, its finest. When buying, always check that it is creamy yellow with delicate green veining. Avoid hard or discolored cheese. It should have a rich, piquant aroma, not a bitter smell. If you find Gorgonzola too strong or rich, you could substitute Danish blue.

gnocchi with tomatoes & herbs

Freshly made potato gnocchi are delicious, especially when they are topped with a fragrant tomato sauce.

Serves 4

12 oz mealy potatoes (those suitable
    for baking or mashing), halved

2¾ oz self-rising flour, plus extra for
    rolling out

2 tsp dried oregano

2 tbsp oil

1 large onion, chopped

2 garlic cloves, chopped

14 oz canned chopped tomatoes

½ vegetable bouillon cube dissolved
    in ½ cup boiling water

salt and pepper

2 tbsp basil, shredded, plus whole leaves
    to garnish

Parmesan cheese, grated, to serve

1 Bring a large pan of water to a boil.
   Add the potatoes and cook for
12–15 minutes, or until tender. Drain and
let cool.

2 Peel and then mash the potatoes
   with the salt and pepper, sifted flour,
and oregano. Mix together with your
hands to form a dough.

3 Heat the oil in a pan. Add the onions
   and garlic and cook for 3–4 minutes.
Add the tomatoes and bouillon, and
cook, uncovered, for 10 minutes.
Season with salt and pepper to taste.

4 Roll the potato dough into a
   sausage about 1 inch in diameter.
Cut the sausage into 1 inch lengths.
Flour your hands, then press a fork into
each piece to create a series of ridges on
one side, and the indent of your index
finger on the other.

5 Bring a large pan of water to a boil
   and cook the gnocchi, in batches,
for 2–3 minutes. They should rise to the
surface when cooked. Drain well and
keep warm.

6 Stir the basil into the tomato sauce
   and pour over the gnocchi. Garnish
with basil leaves and freshly ground
black pepper. Sprinkle with Parmesan
and serve.

2

cook's tip

Try serving the gnocchi with
pesto sauce (see page 23) for
a change.

3

4

spicy pasta wheels

This filling vegetarian dish is perfect for an inexpensive and quick lunch.

Serves 4

5 tbsp olive oil

3 garlic cloves, minced

2 fresh red chiles, chopped

1 green chile, chopped

¼ cup Italian Red Wine Sauce
    (see Cook's Tip)

3½ cups dried rotelle

salt and pepper

warm Italian bread, to serve

1 Make the Italian Red Wine Sauce (see Cook's Tip, right).

2 Heat 4 tbsp of the oil in a saucepan. Add the garlic and chiles and cook for 3 minutes.

3 Stir in the Italian Red Wine Sauce (see Cook's Tip, right) and season with salt and pepper to taste. Simmer gently over a low heat for 20 minutes.

cook's tip

Take care when using fresh chiles, as they can burn your skin. Handle them as little as possible—wear protective gloves. Always wash your hands thoroughly afterward and don't touch your face or eyes before you have washed your hands. Remove chile seeds before chopping the chiles, as they are the hottest part and should not be allowed to slip into the food.

4 Bring a large pan of lightly salted water to a boil. Add the rotelle and the remaining oil and cook for 8 minutes, or until just tender, but still firm to the bite. Drain the pasta.

5 Toss the rotelle in the spicy sauce, then transfer to a warm serving dish. Serve with warm Italian bread.

cook's tip

To make Italian Red Wine Sauce, first make a demi-glace sauce by combining ⅝ cup each Brown bouillon (see page 35) and Espagnole Sauce (see page 39). Cook for 10 minutes, then strain. Meanwhile, combine ½ cup red wine, 2 tbsp red wine vinegar, 4 tbsp chopped shallots, 1 bay leaf, and 1 thyme sprig in a small pan. Bring to a boil and reduce by about three-quarters. Add the demi-glace sauce and simmer for 20 minutes. Season with pepper and strain.

2

3

5

crispy golden seafood

Deep-fried seafood is popular all around the Mediterranean, where fish of all kinds is fresh and abundant. Serve with garlic mayonnaise and lemon wedges.

Serves 4

7 oz prepared squid

7 oz raw jumbo shrimp, peeled

5½ oz whitebait

oil, for deep-frying

1½ oz all-purpose flour

1 tsp dried basil

salt and pepper

TO SERVE

garlic mayonnaise (see Cook's Tip)

lemon wedges

1 Carefully rinse the squid, shrimp, and whitebait under cold running water, completely removing any dirt or grit.

2 Using a sharp knife, slice the squid into thin rings, leaving the tentacles whole.

3 Heat the oil in a large saucepan to 350°–375°F or until a cube of bread browns in 30 seconds.

4 Place the flour in a bowl and season with the salt, pepper, and basil.

5 Roll the squid, shrimp, and whitebait in the seasoned flour until coated all over. Carefully shake off any excess flour.

6 Cook the seafood in the heated oil in batches for 2–3 minutes, or until crispy and golden all over. Remove all of the seafood with a draining spoon and let drain thoroughly on kitchen paper.

7 Transfer the deep-fried seafood to serving plates and serve with garlic mayonnaise (see Cook's Tip) and lemon wedges.

5

6

2

cook's tip

To make garlic mayonnaise for serving with the deep-fried seafood, crush 2 garlic cloves, stir into 8 tablespoons of mayonnaise, then season with salt and pepper and a little chopped parsley.

polenta skewers with prosciutto

Here, skewers of thyme-flavored polenta, wrapped in prosciutto, are broiled or grilled.

Serves 4

6 oz instant polenta

scant 3¾ cups water

2 tbsp fresh thyme, stalks removed

8 slices prosciutto (about 2¾ oz)

1 tbsp olive oil

salt and pepper

fresh green salad, to serve

1 Cook the polenta, using 3¾ cups of water to 6 oz polenta, stirring occasionally. Alternatively, follow the instructions on the package.

2 Add the fresh thyme to the polenta mixture and season to taste with salt and pepper.

3 Spread out the polenta, about 1 inch thick, on to a board. Set aside to cool.

4 Using a sharp knife, cut the cooled polenta into 1-inch cubes.

5 Cut the prosciutto slices into 2 pieces lengthwise. Wrap the prosciutto around the polenta cubes.

6 Thread the prosciutto wrapped polenta cubes onto skewers.

7 Brush the kabobs with oil and cook under a preheated broiler, turning frequently, for 7–8 minutes. Alternatively, grill the kabobs until golden. Transfer to serving plates and serve with a green salad.

5

4

6

cook's tip

Try flavoring the polenta with chopped oregano, basil, or marjoram instead of the thyme, if you prefer. You should use 1 tablespoon of chopped herbs to every 4 oz instant polenta.

creamy bacon spaghetti

Ensure that all of the cooked ingredients are as hot as possible before adding the eggs, so they cook on contact.

Serves 4

15 oz dried spaghetti

2 tbsp olive oil

1 large onion, thinly sliced

2 garlic cloves, chopped

6 oz rindless bacon, cut into

    thin strips

2 tbsp butter

6 oz mushrooms, thinly sliced

1¼ cups heavy cream

3 eggs, beaten

1 cup freshly grated Parmesan cheese,

    plus extra to serve (optional)

salt and pepper

fresh sage sprigs, to garnish

2

3

4

cook's tip

The key to success with this recipe is not to overcook the egg. That is why it is important to keep all the ingredients hot enough just to cook the egg—work rapidly to avoid scrambling it.

1 Warm a large serving dish or bowl. Bring a large pan of lightly salted water to a boil. Add the spaghetti and 1 tbsp of the oil and cook until tender but still firm to the bite. Drain, return to the pan, and keep warm.

2 Meanwhile, heat the remaining oil in a skillet over a medium heat. Add the onion and cook until it is transparent. Add the garlic and bacon and cook until the bacon is crisp. Transfer to the warm plate.

3 Melt the butter in the skillet. Add the mushrooms and fry, stirring occasionally, for 3–4 minutes. Return the bacon mixture to the pan. Cover and keep warm.

4 Mix together the cream, eggs, and cheese in a large bowl and then season to taste with salt and pepper.

5 Working very quickly, tip the spaghetti into the bacon and mushroom mixture and pour over the eggs. Toss the spaghetti quickly into the egg and cream mixture, using 2 forks, and serve at once. If you wish, serve with extra grated Parmesan cheese.

pasta with ham & italian cheese sauce

Served with freshly made Italian bread or tossed with pesto, this makes a mouthwatering light lunch.

Serves 4

1 lb dried linguini

1 lb green broccoli flowerets

8 oz Italian smoked ham

⅝ cup Italian Cheese Sauce (see Cook's Tip, below)

salt and pepper

Italian bread, to serve

1 Bring a large pan of lightly salted water to a boil. Add the linguini and broccoli flowerets and cook for 10 minutes, or until the linguini is tender, but still firm to the bite.

2 Drain the linguini and broccoli thoroughly, then set aside and keep warm.

3 Meanwhile, make the Italian Cheese Sauce (see Cook's Tip, below left).

4 Cut the Italian smoked ham into thin strips. Toss the linguini, broccoli, and ham into the Italian Cheese Sauce and gently warm through over a low heat.

5 Transfer the pasta mixture to a warm serving dish. Sprinkle with black pepper and serve with Italian bread.

1

4

4

cook's tip

For Italian Cheese Sauce, melt 2 tbsp butter in a pan and stir in ¼ cup all-purpose flour. Cook, stirring, over a low heat until the roux is light in color and crumbly in texture. Stir in 1¼ cups hot milk. Cook, stirring, for 15 minutes, or until thick and smooth. Add a pinch of nutmeg, a pinch of dried thyme, 2 tbsp white wine vinegar, and seasoning. Stir in 3 tbsp heavy cream and mix. Stir in ½ cup grated mozzarella cheese, ⅔ cup grated Parmesan cheese, 1 tsp English mustard, and 2 tbsp sour cream.

cook's tip

There are many types of Italian bread which would be suitable to serve with this dish. Ciabatta is made with olive oil and is available plain and with different ingredients, such as olives or sun-dried tomatoes.

potato salad with sun-dried tomatoes

Potato salad is always a favorite, but it is even more delicious with the addition of sun-dried tomatoes and fresh parsley.

Serves 4

1 lb baby potatoes, unpeeled, or larger
    potatoes, halved

8 sun-dried tomatoes

4 tbsp unsweetened yogurt

4 tbsp mayonnaise

2 tbsp flatleaf parsley, chopped

salt and pepper

cook's tip

It is easier to cut the larger potatoes once they are cooked. Although smaller pieces of potato will cook more quickly, they tend to disintegrate and become mushy.

1 Rinse and clean the potatoes and place them in a large pan of water. Bring to a boil and cook for 8–12 minutes, or until just tender. (The cooking time will vary according to the size of your potatoes.)

2 Using a sharp knife, cut the sun-dried tomatoes into thin slices.

3 To make the dressing, mix together the yogurt and mayonnaise in a bowl and season to taste with a little salt and pepper. Stir in the sun-dried tomato slices and the chopped flatleaf parsley.

4 Remove the potatoes with a draining spoon and drain them thoroughly, then set them aside to cool. If you are using larger potatoes, cut them into 2 inch chunks.

5 Pour the dressing over the potatoes and toss to mix.

6 Leave the potato salad to chill in the refrigerator for about 20 minutes, then serve as an appetizer or as an accompaniment.

1

2

3

sicilian eggplant salad

This cooked salad from Sicily was first brought to Italy by the Moors.

1

2

4

Serves 4

6 tbsp olive oil

1 onion, chopped

2 garlic cloves, chopped

2 celery stalks, chopped

1 lb eggplant

14 oz canned tomatoes, chopped

1¼ oz green olives, stoned and chopped

1 oz granulated sugar

2¼ cups red wine vinegar

1 oz capers, drained

salt and pepper

1 tbsp flatleaf parsley, coarsely chopped,
    to garnish

1 Heat 2 tablespoons of the oil in a large skillet. Add the prepared onions, garlic, and celery to the skillet and cook, stirring, for 3–4 minutes.

2 Using a sharp knife, slice the eggplant into thick rounds, then cut each round into 4 pieces.

3 Add the eggplant pieces to the skillet with the remaining olive oil and cook for 5 minutes, or until golden.

4 Add the tomatoes, olives, and sugar to the pan, stirring until the sugar has dissolved.

5 Add the red wine vinegar, then reduce the heat, and let simmer for 10–15 minutes, or until the sauce is thick and the eggplant are tender.

6 While the pan is still on the heat, stir in the capers. Season to taste with salt and pepper.

7 Transfer to serving plates and garnish with the chopped fresh flatleaf parsley.

cook's tip

This salad is best served cold the day after it is made, which lets the flavors mingle and be fully absorbed.

macaroni & cabbage salad

This crunchy, colorful salad would be a good accompaniment for any broiled meat or fish dish.

Serves 4

2¼ cups dried short-cut macaroni

5 tbsp olive oil

1 large red cabbage, shredded

1 large white cabbage, shredded

2 large apples, diced

9 oz cooked smoked bacon or ham, diced

8 tbsp wine vinegar

1 tbsp sugar

salt and pepper

2

4

1 Bring a large saucepan of lightly salted water to a boil. Add the macaroni and 1 tbsp of the olive oil and cook until tender, but still firm to the bite. Drain the pasta, then refresh in cold water. Drain the pasta again and set aside.

2 Bring a large saucepan of lightly salted water to a boil. Add the shredded red cabbage and cook for 5 minutes. Drain thoroughly and set aside to cool.

3 Bring a large saucepan of lightly salted water to a boil. Add the white cabbage and cook for 5 minutes. Drain thoroughly and set aside to cool.

4 In a large bowl, mix together the pasta, red cabbage, and apple. In a separate bowl, mix together the white cabbage and bacon or ham.

5 In a small bowl, mix together the remaining oil, the vinegar, and sugar, then season to taste with salt and pepper. Pour the dressing over each of the 2 cabbage mixtures and, finally, mix them all together. Serve immediately.

5

variation

Alternative dressings for this salad can be made with 4 tbsp olive oil, 4 tbsp red wine, 4 tbsp red wine vinegar, and 1 tbsp sugar. Or you could substitute 3 tbsp olive oil and 1 tbsp walnut or hazelnut oil for the olive oil.

penne, apple & walnut salad

This crisp salad would make an excellent accompaniment to broiled meat and is ideal for summer barbecues.

Serves 4

2 large lettuces

9 oz dried penne

1 tbsp olive oil

8 red eating apples

juice of 4 lemons

1 head of celery, sliced

¾ cup shelled, halved walnuts

1¼ cups fresh garlic mayonnaise
 (see Cook's Tip, right)

salt

1 Wash, drain, and pat dry the lettuce leaves with paper towels. Transfer them to the refrigerator for 1 hour, until crisp.

2 Meanwhile, bring a large saucepan of lightly salted water to a boil. Add the pasta and olive oil and cook until tender, but still firm to the bite. Drain the pasta and refresh under cold running water. Drain thoroughly and set aside.

3 Core and dice the apples, then place them in a small bowl and sprinkle with the lemon juice. Mix together the pasta, celery, apples, and walnuts and toss the mixture in the garlic mayonnaise (see Cook's Tip, right). Add more mayonnaise, if liked.

4 Line a salad bowl with the lettuce leaves and spoon the pasta salad into the lined bowl. Serve when required.

variation

Sprinkling the apples with lemon juice will prevent them from turning brown.

cook's tip

To make homemade garlic mayonnaise, beat 2 egg yolks with a pinch of salt and 6 minced garlic cloves. Start beating in 1½ cups olive oil, 1-2 tsp at a time, using a balloon whisk or electric mixer. When about one quarter of the oil has been incorporated, beat in 1-2 tbsp white wine vinegar. Continue beating in the oil, adding it in a thin, continuous stream. Finally, stir in 1 tsp Dijon mustard and season to taste with salt and pepper.

1

3

3

warm beet salad

Quick and simple, this colorful, warm salad works equally well as a tasty appetizer or as a main dish.

Serves 4

11 oz dried ditalini rigati

5 tbsp olive oil

2 garlic cloves, chopped

14 oz canned chopped tomatoes

14 oz cooked beet, diced

2 tbsp chopped fresh basil leaves

1 tsp mustard seeds

salt and pepper

TO SERVE

mixed salad greens, tossed in olive oil

4 Italian plum tomatoes, sliced

2

2

3

1 Bring a large saucepan of lightly salted water to a boil. Add the pasta and 1 tbsp of the oil and cook for about 10 minutes, or until tender, but still firm to the bite. Drain the pasta thoroughly and set aside.

2 Heat the remaining olive oil in a large saucepan. Add the garlic and cook for 3 minutes. Add the chopped tomatoes and cook for 10 minutes.

3 Remove the pan from the heat and carefully add the beet, basil, mustard seeds, and pasta and season to taste with salt and black pepper.

4 Serve on a bed of mixed salad greens tossed in olive oil, and sliced plum tomatoes.

cook's tip

To cook raw beetroot, trim off the leaves about 2 inches above the root and ensure that the skin is not broken. Boil in lightly salted water for 30-40 minutes, or until tender. Leave to cool and rub off the skin.

cook's tip

Mustard seeds come from three different plants and may be black, brown or white. Black and brown mustard seeds have a stronger, more pungent flavour than white mustard.

goat cheese & pasta salad

This superb salad was created especially to accompany venison cooked in Chablis, but is equally delicious with other strongly flavored meat dishes.

Serves 4

9 oz dried penne

5 tbsp olive oil

1 head radicchio, torn into pieces

1 Webbs lettuce, torn into pieces

7 tbsp chopped walnuts

2 ripe pears, cored and diced

1 fresh basil sprig

1 bunch of watercress, trimmed

2 tbsp lemon juice

3 tbsp garlic vinegar

4 tomatoes, cut into fourths

1 small onion, sliced

1 large carrot, grated

9 oz goat cheese, diced

salt and pepper

1 Bring a large saucepan of lightly salted water to a boil. Add the penne and 1 tbsp of the olive oil and cook until tender, but still firm to the bite. Drain the pasta and refresh under cold running water, then drain thoroughly again and set aside to cool.

2 Place the radicchio and Webbs lettuce in a large salad bowl and mix together well. Top with the pasta, walnuts, pears, basil, and watercress.

3 Mix together the lemon juice, the remaining olive oil, and the vinegar in a measuring pitcher. Pour the mixture over the salad ingredients and toss to coat the salad leaves well.

cook's tip

Most goat cheese comes from France and there are many varieties, such as Crottin de Chavignol, Chabi, which is very pungent, and Sainte-Maure, which is available in creamery and farmhouse varieties.

4 Add the tomato fourths, onion slices, grated carrot, and diced goat cheese and toss together, using 2 forks, until well mixed. Let the salad chill in the refrigerator for about 1 hour before serving.

2

2

3

pasta & avocado salad

Tomatoes and mozzarella cheese are a classic Italian combination. Here they are joined with pasta spirals and avocado pear for an extra touch of luxury.

3

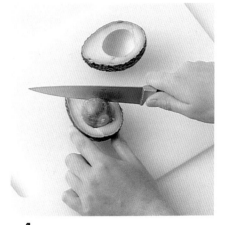

4

5

Serves 4

2 tbsp pine kernels

1½ cups dried fusilli

1 tbsp olive oil

6 tomatoes

8 oz mozzarella cheese

1 large avocado pear

2 tbsp lemon juice

3 tbsp chopped fresh basil

salt and pepper

fresh basil sprigs, to garnish

DRESSING

6 tbsp extra virgin olive oil

2 tbsp white wine vinegar

1 tsp wholegrain mustard

pinch of sugar

1 Spread the pine kernels out on a cookie sheet and toast under a preheated broiler for 1–2 minutes. Remove and set aside to cool.

2 Bring a large saucepan of lightly salted water to a boil. Add the fusilli and olive oil and cook until tender, but still firm to the bite. Drain the pasta and refresh in cold water. Drain again and set aside to cool.

3 Thinly slice the tomatoes and the mozzarella cheese.

4 Cut the avocado pear in half, then remove the pit and skin. Cut into thin slices lengthwise and sprinkle with lemon juice to prevent discoloration.

5 To make the dressing, whisk together the oil, vinegar, mustard, and sugar in a small bowl, and season to taste with salt and black pepper.

6 Arrange the tomatoes, mozzarella cheese, and avocado pear alternately in overlapping slices on a platter.

7 Toss the pasta with half of the dressing and the chopped basil and season to taste with salt and black pepper. Spoon the pasta into the center of the platter and pour over the remaining dressing. Sprinkle over the pine kernels and garnish with fresh basil sprigs, then serve immediately.

fusilli salad with chile

This roasted pepper and chile sauce is sweet and spicy.

Serves 4

2 red bell peppers, halved and seeded

1 small red chile

2 garlic cloves

4 tomatoes, halved

1¼ oz ground almonds

7 tbsp olive oil

1 lb 8 oz fresh pasta or 12 oz dried pasta

fresh oregano leaves, to garnish

1 Place the bell peppers, skin-side up, on a cookie sheet with the chile and garlic. Cook under a preheated broiler for 15 minutes, or until charred. After 10 minutes, turn the tomatoes skin-side up.

2 Place the bell peppers and chile in a plastic bag and let them sweat for 10 minutes.

3 Remove the skin from the bell peppers and chile and slice the flesh into strips, using a sharp knife.

4 Peel the garlic and peel and seed the tomatoes.

5 Place the almonds on a cookie sheet and place under the broiler for 2–3 minutes, or until golden.

6 Using a food processor, blend the bell pepper, chile, garlic, and tomatoes to make a paste. Keep the motor running and slowly add the olive oil to form a thick sauce. Alternatively, mash the mixture with a fork and beat in the olive oil, drop by drop.

7 Stir the toasted ground almonds into the mixture.

8 Warm the sauce in a pan until it is heated through.

9 Cook the pasta in a pan of boiling water according to the instructions on the packet or until it is cooked through,.but still has bite. Drain the pasta and transfer to a serving dish. Pour over the sauce and toss to mix. Garnish with fresh oregano leaves.

1

3

variation

Add 2 tablespoons of red wine vinegar to the sauce and use as a dressing for a cold pasta salad, if you wish.

5

conchiglie & walnut salad

Use colorful salad greens to provide visual contrast to match the contrasts of taste and texture.

Serves 4

2 cups dried pasta shells

1 tbsp olive oil

1 cup shelled and halved walnuts

mixed salad greens, such as radicchio, escarole, arugula, corn salad, and frisée

8 oz dolcelatte cheese, crumbled

salt

DRESSING

2 tbsp walnut oil

4 tbsp extra-virgin olive oil

2 tbsp red wine vinegar

salt and pepper

1 Bring a large saucepan of lightly salted water to a boil. Add the pasta shells and olive oil and cook until just tender, but still firm to the bite. Drain the pasta and refresh under cold running water, drain thoroughly again and set aside.

2 Spread out the shelled walnut halves on to a cookie sheet and toast under a preheated broiler for 2–3 minutes. Let cool while you make the dressing.

3 To make the dressing, whisk together the walnut oil, olive oil, and vinegar in a small bowl, and season to taste with salt and black pepper.

4 Arrange the salad greens in a large serving bowl. Pile the cooled pasta in the middle of the salad greens and sprinkle over the dolcelatte cheese. Pour the dressing over the pasta salad, then scatter over the walnut halves and toss together to mix. Serve immediately.

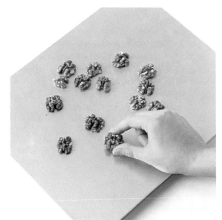

2

3

3

cook's tip

Dolcelatte is a semi-soft, blue-veined cheese from Italy. Its texture is creamy and smooth and the flavor is delicate, but piquant. You could substitute Roquefort as an alternative. Whichever cheese you choose, it is essential that it is of the best quality and in peak condition.

niçoise salad italian-style

This is a more filling variation on the traditional Niçoise salad from southern France.

Serves 4

3 cups dried small pasta shells

1 tbsp olive oil

4 oz green beans

1¾ oz canned anchovies, drained

⅛ cup milk

2 small crisp lettuces

1 lb or 3 large beef tomatoes

4 hard-cooked eggs

8 oz canned tuna, drained

1 cup pitted black olives

salt and pepper

VINAIGRETTE DRESSING

¼ cup extra-virgin olive oil

2 tbsp white wine vinegar

1 tsp wholegrain mustard

salt and pepper

1 Bring a large saucepan of lightly salted water to a boil. Add the pasta and the olive oil and cook until tender, but still firm to the bite. Drain and refresh in cold water.

2 Bring a small saucepan of lightly salted water to a boil. Add the beans and cook for 10–12 minutes, or until tender, but still firm to the bite. Drain and refresh in cold water, then drain thoroughly once more and set aside.

3 Put the anchovies in a shallow bowl, then pour over the milk and set aside for 10 minutes. Meanwhile, tear the lettuces into large pieces. Blanch the tomatoes in boiling water for 1–2 minutes, then drain. Skin and coarsely chop the flesh. Shell the eggs and cut into fourths. Cut the tuna into large chunks.

4 Drain the anchovies and the pasta. Put all of the salad ingredients, the beans, and the olives into a large bowl and gently mix together.

5 To make the vinaigrette dressing, beat together all the dressing ingredients and keep in the refrigerator until required. Just before serving, pour the vinaigrette dressing over the salad.

cook's tip

It is very convenient to make salad dressings in a screw-top jar. Put all the ingredients in the jar, then cover securely and shake well to mix and emulsify the oil.

3

3

3

mixed seafood & pasta salad

This delicious mix of seafood, salad greens, and ripe tomatoes conjures up all the warmth and sunshine of Naples.

Serves 4

1 lb prepared squid, cut into strips

1 lb 10 oz cooked mussels

1 lb cooked cockles in brine

⅝ cup white wine

1¼ cups olive oil

2 cups dried campanelle or other small
    pasta shapes

juice of 1 lemon

1 bunch chives, snipped

1 bunch fresh parsley, finely chopped

4 large tomatoes, cut into fourths or sliced

mixed salad greens

salt and pepper

sprig of fresh basil, to garnish

1

4

5

variation

You can substitute cooked scallops for the mussels and clams in brine for the cockles.

1 Put all of the seafood into a large bowl. Pour over the wine and half the olive oil, then set aside for 6 hours.

2 Put the seafood mixture into a saucepan and simmer over a low heat for 10 minutes. Set aside to cool.

3 Bring a large saucepan of lightly salted water to a boil. Add the pasta and 1 tbsp of the remaining olive oil and cook until tender, but still firm to the bite. Drain thoroughly and refresh in cold water.

4 Strain off about half of the cooking liquid from the seafood and discard the rest. Mix in the lemon juice, chives, parsley, and the remaining olive oil. Season to taste with salt and pepper. Drain the pasta and add to the seafood.

5 Cut the tomatoes into fourths. Shred the salad greens and arrange them at the base of a salad bowl. Spoon in the seafood salad and garnish with the tomatoes and a sprig of basil.

herring, conchiglie & apple salad

This salad, which so many countries claim as their own, is considered in Holland to be a typically Dutch dish.

Serves 4

2¼ cups dried pasta shells

5 tbsp olive oil

14 oz rollmop herrings in brine

6 boiled potatoes

2 large tart apples

2 baby frisée lettuces

2 baby beet

4 hard-cooked eggs

6 pickled onions

6 dill pickles

2 tbsp capers

3 tbsp of tarragon vinegar

salt and pepper

1 Bring a large saucepan of lightly salted water to a boil. Add the pasta and 1 tbsp of the olive oil and cook until tender, but still firm to the bite. Drain the pasta thoroughly and then refresh in cold running water.

2 Cut the herrings, potatoes, apples, frisée lettuces, and beet into small pieces. Put all of these ingredients into a large salad bowl.

3 Drain the pasta thoroughly and add to the salad bowl. Toss lightly to mix the pasta and herring mixture together.

2

4 Carefully shell and slice the eggs. Garnish the salad with the slices of egg, pickled onions, dill pickles, and capers, then sprinkle with the remaining olive oil and the tarragon vinegar and serve immediately.

cook's tip

Tarragon vinegar is available from most supermarkets, but you can easily make your own. Add a bunch of fresh tarragon to a bottle of white or red wine vinegar and let stand to infuse for 48 hours. It is important to ensure that the tarragon is as fresh as possible and to discard any blemished leaves.

cook's tip

Store this salad, without the dressing, in a container in the refrigerator.

2

3

spiced tuna salad

In this recipe, lentils, combined with spices, lemon juice, and tuna, make a wonderfully tasty and filling salad.

Serves 4

3 tbsp virgin olive oil

1 tbsp lemon juice

1 tsp wholegrain mustard

1 garlic clove, minced

½ tsp cumin powder

½ tsp ground coriander

2 ripe tomatoes

1 small red onion

14 oz canned lentils, drained

6½ oz canned tuna, drained

2 tbsp fresh cilantro, chopped

pepper

variation

Nuts would add extra flavor and texture to this salad.

1 To make the dressing, whisk together the virgin olive oil, lemon juice, mustard, garlic, cumin powder, and ground coriander in a small bowl. Set aside until required.

2 Using a sharp knife, seed the tomatoes and chop them into fine dice.

3 Using a sharp knife, finely chop the red onion.

4 Mix together the chopped onion, diced tomatoes, and drained lentils in a large bowl.

5 Flake the tuna and stir it into the onion, tomato, and lentil mixture.

6 Stir in the chopped fresh cilantro.

7 Pour the dressing over the lentil and tuna salad and season with freshly ground black pepper. Serve at once.

cook's tip

Lentils are a good source of protein and contain important vitamins and minerals. Buy them dried for soaking and cooking yourself, or buy canned varieties for speed and convenience.

1

2

4

Pasta and meat or poultry is a classic combination. Dishes range from easy, economic mid-week suppers to sophisticated and elegant meals for special occasions. The recipes in this chapter include many family favourites, such as Spaghetti Bolognese, Meatball Pasta with Tarragon, Lasagna with Meat Sauce & Herbs, and Spinach & Ricotta Cannelloni. There are also some exciting variations on traditional themes, such as Beef & Eggplant

Pasta, Creamy Beef Macaroni and Mediterranean Chicken & Mixed Peppers. Finally, there is a superb collection of mouthwatering original recipes. Why not try Prawn-stuffed Chicken on Tagliatelle, Creamy Pork & Quail Egg Pasta, Duck with Raspberry & Honey or Lime Partridge with Pesto.

poultry
game&
meat

chicken tortellini with creamy mushroom sauce

Tortellini were said to have been created in the image of the goddess Venus's navel. Whatever the story, these delicate filled pasta swirls offer a delicious blend of Italian flavors.

chicken lasagna with prosciutto & marsala

You can use your favorite mushrooms, such as chanterelles or oyster mushrooms, for this delicately flavored dish.

Serves 4

butter, for greasing

14 sheets pre-cooked lasagna

3¾ cups Béchamel Sauce

1 cup grated Parmesan cheese

CHICKEN & EXOTIC MUSHROOM SAUCE

2 tbsp olive oil

2 garlic cloves, minced

1 large onion, finely chopped

8 oz exotic mushrooms, sliced

2½ cups ground chicken

3 oz chicken livers, finely chopped

4 oz prosciutto, diced

⅝ cup Marsala wine

10 oz canned chopped tomatoes

1 tbsp chopped fresh basil leaves

2 tbsp tomato paste

salt and pepper

1 To make the chicken and wild mushroom sauce, heat the olive oil in a large pan. Add the garlic, onion, and mushrooms and cook, stirring frequently, for 6 minutes.

2 Add the ground chicken, chicken livers, and prosciutto and cook over a low heat for 12 minutes.

3 Stir the Marsala wine, tomatoes, basil, and tomato paste into the mixture in the pan and cook for 4 minutes. Season to taste with salt and pepper, then cover and simmer for 30 minutes. Uncover the pan, stir, and simmer for an additional 15 minutes.

2

4 Lightly grease an ovenproof dish with butter. Arrange sheets of lasagna over the base of the dish then spoon over a layer of Chicken and Exotic Mushroom Sauce, then spoon over a layer of Béchamel Sauce. Place another layer of lasagna on top and repeat the process twice, finishing with a layer of Béchamel Sauce. Sprinkle over the grated cheese and bake in a preheated oven at 375°F for 35 minutes, or until golden brown and bubbling. Serve immediately.

3

4

italian broiled chicken & pesto bread

This Italian-style dish is richly flavored with pesto, which is a mixture of basil, olive oil, pine nuts, and Parmesan cheese. Either red or green pesto can be used for this recipe.

Serves 4

8 part-boned chicken thighs

olive oil, for brushing

1⅔ cups strained tomatoes

½ cup green or red pesto sauce

12 slices French bread

1 cup freshly grated Parmesan cheese

½ cup pine nuts or slivered almonds

basil sprig, to garnish

1 Arrange the chicken in a single layer in a wide flameproof dish and brush lightly with oil. Place under a preheated broiler for about 15 minutes, turning occasionally until golden brown.

2 Pierce with a skewer to ensure that there is no trace of pink in the chicken juices.

3 Pour off any excess fat. Warm the strained tomatoes and half the pesto sauce in a small pan and pour over the chicken. Broil for a few more minutes, turning until coated.

4 Meanwhile, spread the remaining pesto on to the slices of bread. Arrange the bread over the chicken and sprinkle with the Parmesan cheese. Scatter the pine nuts over the cheese. Broil for 2–3 minutes, or until browned and bubbling. Serve hot, garnished with a basil sprig.

1

cook's tip

Leaving the skin on means the chicken will have a higher fat content, but many people like the rich taste and crispy skin, especially when it is blackened by the broiler. The skin also keeps in the cooking juices.

2

4

apulian olive chicken in white wine

Olives are a popular flavoring for poultry and game in the Apulia region of Italy, where this recipe originates.

1

2

3

Serves 4

3 tbsp olive oil

2 tbsp butter

4 chicken breasts, part boned

1 large onion, finely chopped

2 garlic cloves, minced

2 red, yellow, or green bell peppers, cored, seeded, and cut into large pieces

9 oz white mushrooms, sliced or cut into fourths

6 oz tomatoes, skinned and halved

⁄ cup dry white wine

1 ⁄ cups pitted green olives

4–6 tbsp heavy cream

14 oz dried pasta

salt and pepper

chopped flatleaf parsley, to garnish

1 Heat 2 tbsp of the oil and the butter in a skillet. Add the chicken breasts and cook until golden brown all over. Remove the chicken from the skillet.

2 Add the onion and garlic to the skillet and cook over a medium heat until beginning to soften. Add the bell peppers and mushrooms and cook for 2–3 minutes. Add the tomatoes and season to taste with salt and pepper. Transfer the vegetables to a casserole and arrange the chicken on top.

3 Add the wine to the pan and bring to a boil. Pour the wine over the chicken. Cover and cook in a preheated oven at 350°F for 50 minutes.

4 Add the olives to the casserole and mix in. Pour in the cream, then cover and return to the oven for an additional 10–20 minutes.

5 Meanwhile, bring a large pan of lightly salted water to a boil. Add the pasta and the remaining oil and cook until tender, but still firm to the bite. Drain the pasta and transfer to a serving dish.

6 Arrange the chicken on top of the pasta, then spoon over the sauce and garnish with the parsley, and serve immediately. Alternatively, place the pasta in a large serving bowl and serve separately.

stuffed chicken parcels

Stuffed with creamy ricotta, nutmeg, and spinach, then wrapped with wafer-thin slices of prosciutto and gently cooked in white wine.

Serves 4

½ cup frozen spinach, defrosted

½ cup ricotta cheese

pinch grated nutmeg

4 skinless, boneless chicken breasts,
    each weighing 6 oz

4 prosciutto slices

2 tbsp butter

1 tbsp olive oil

12 small onions or shallots

1½ cups white mushrooms, sliced

1 tbsp all-purpose flour

⅔ cup dry white or red wine

1¼ cups chicken bouillon

salt and pepper

2

3

4

1 Put the spinach into a strainer and press out the water with a spoon. Mix with the ricotta and nutmeg and season with salt and pepper to taste.

2 Using a sharp knife, slit each chicken breast through the side and enlarge each cut to form a pocket. Fill with the spinach mixture, then reshape the chicken breasts. Wrap each breast tightly in a slice of prosciutto and secure with toothpicks. Cover and chill in the refrigerator.

3 Heat the butter and oil in a skillet and brown the chicken breasts for 2 minutes on each side. Transfer the chicken to a large, shallow ovenproof dish and keep warm until required.

4 Cook the onions and mushrooms for 2–3 minutes, until lightly browned. Stir in the all-purpose flour, then gradually add the wine and bouillon. Bring to a boil, stirring constantly. Season and spoon the mixture around the chicken.

5 Cook the chicken uncovered in a preheated oven, 400°F, for 20 minutes. Turn the breasts over and cook for an additional 10 minutes. Remove the toothpick and serve with the sauce, together with carrot purée and green beans, if wished.

cheese-stuffed chicken in white wine

There is a delicious surprise inside these chicken breast packets!

Serves 4

4 chicken breasts, skin removed

3½ oz full-fat soft cheese, flavored with
    herbs and garlic

8 slices prosciutto

⅓ cup red wine

⅔ cup chicken bouillon

1 tbsp brown sugar

variation

Try adding 2 finely chopped
sun-dried tomatoes to the soft
cheese in step 2, if you
prefer.

1 Using a sharp knife, make a horizontal slit along the length of each chicken breast to form a pocket.

2 Beat the cheese with a wooden spoon to soften it. Spoon the cheese into the pocket of the chicken breasts.

3 Wrap 2 slices of prosciutto around each chicken breast and secure in place with string.

4 Pour the wine and chicken bouillon into a large skillet and bring to a boil. When the mixture is just starting to boil, add the sugar and stir to dissolve.

5 Add the chicken breasts to the mixture in the skillet. Let simmer for 12–15 minutes, or until the chicken is tender and the juices run clear when a skewer is inserted into the thickest part of the meat.

6 Remove the chicken from the pan, then set aside and keep warm.

7 Reheat the sauce and boil until reduced and thickened. Remove the string from the chicken and cut into slices. Pour the sauce over the chicken to serve.

1

2

3

lemon chicken conchiglie

Chicken pieces are cooked in a succulent, lemon and mild mustard sauce, then coated in poppy seeds and served on a bed of fresh pasta shells.

1

3

3

Serves 4

8 chicken pieces (about 4 oz each)

4 tbsp butter, melted

4 tbsp mild mustard (see Cook's Tip)

2 tbsp lemon juice

1 tbsp brown sugar

1 tsp paprika

3 tbsp poppy seeds

14 oz fresh pasta shells

1 tbsp olive oil

salt and pepper

1 Arrange the chicken pieces, smooth side down, in a single layer in a large ovenproof dish.

2 Mix together the butter, mustard, lemon juice, sugar, and paprika in a bowl and season to taste with salt and pepper. Brush the mixture over the upper surfaces of the chicken pieces and bake in a preheated oven at 400°F for 15 minutes.

3 Remove the dish from the oven and carefully turn over the chicken pieces. Coat the upper surfaces of the chicken with the remaining mustard mixture, then sprinkle the chicken pieces with poppy seeds and return to the oven for an additional 15 minutes.

4 Meanwhile, bring a large pan of lightly salted water to a boil. Add the pasta shells and olive oil and cook until tender, but still firm to the bite.

5 Drain the pasta and arrange on a warmed serving dish. Top with the chicken, pour over the sauce and serve immediately.

cook's tip

Dijon is the type of mustard most often used in cooking, as it has a clean and only mildly spicy flavor. German mustard has a sweet-sour taste, with Bavarian mustard being slightly sweeter. American mustard is mild and sweet.

Serves 4

1 chicken, weighing about 5 lb

8 slices Mortadella or salami

2 cups fresh white or brown bread crumbs

1 cup freshly grated Parmesan cheese

2 garlic cloves, minced

6 tbsp chopped fresh basil or parsley

1 egg, beaten

pepper

fresh spring vegetables, to serve

1 Bone the chicken, keeping the skin intact. Dislocate each leg by breaking it at the thigh joint. Cut down each side of the backbone, taking care not to pierce the breast skin.

2 Pull the backbone clear of the flesh and discard. Remove the ribs, carefully severing any attached flesh with a sharp knife.

3 Scrape the flesh from each leg and cut away the bone at the joint with a knife or shears.

4 Use the bones for bouillon. Lay out the boned chicken on a board, skin-side down. Arrange the Mortadella slices over the chicken, overlapping slightly.

5 Put the bread crumbs, Parmesan, garlic, and basil or parsley in a bowl. Season well with pepper and mix. Stir in the beaten egg to bind the mixture together. Pile the mixture down the middle of the boned chicken, then roll the meat around it and tie securely with fine cotton string.

6 Place in a roasting dish and brush lightly with olive oil. Roast in a preheated oven, 400°F, for 1½ hours or until the juices run clear when pierced.

7 Serve hot or cold, in slices, with fresh spring vegetables.

variation

Replace the Mortadella with strips of lean bacon, if preferred.

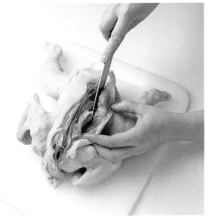

1

2

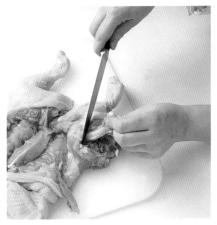

3

stuffed chicken fusilli

Steaming lets you cook without fat, and these little foil packages retain all the natural juices of the chicken while cooking conveniently over the pasta while it boils.

Serves 4

4 skinless, boneless, chicken breasts

1 cup fresh basil leaves

2 tbsp hazelnuts

1 garlic clove, minced

2 cups whole-wheat pasta spirals

2 sun-dried tomatoes or fresh tomatoes

1 tbsp lemon juice

1 tbsp olive oil

1 tbsp capers

⁄ cup black olives

salt and pepper

1 Beat the chicken breasts with a rolling pin to flatten evenly.

2 Process the basil and hazelnuts in a food processor until finely chopped. Mix with the garlic, salt, and pepper.

3 Spread the basil mixture over the chicken breasts and roll up from one short end to enclose the filling. Wrap the chicken roll tightly in foil so that they hold their shape, then seal the ends well.

4 Bring a large pan of lightly salted water to a boil and cook the pasta until tender, but still firm to the bite.

2

3

5 Place the chicken parcels in a steamer basket or colander set over the pan. Cover tightly and steam for 10 minutes. Meanwhile, dice the tomatoes.

6

6 Drain the pasta and return to the pan with the lemon juice, olive oil, tomatoes, capers, and olives. Heat through gently.

7 Pierce the chicken with a skewer to make sure that the juices run clear and not pink, then slice the chicken and arrange over the pasta. Serve.

variation

Sun-dried tomatoes have a wonderful, rich flavor; if you can't find them, use fresh tomatoes.

caramelized chicken in wine

A rich caramelized sauce, flavored with balsamic vinegar and wine, gives this chicken dish a piquant flavor.

1

2

4

Serves 4

4 chicken thighs, boned

2 garlic cloves, minced

¾ cup red wine

3 tbsp white wine vinegar

1 tbsp oil

1 tbsp butter

4 shallots

3 tbsp balsamic vinegar

2 tbsp fresh thyme

salt and pepper

cooked polenta or rice, to serve

1 Using a sharp knife, make a few slashes in the skin of the chicken. Brush the chicken with the minced garlic and place in a non-metallic dish.

2 Pour the wine and white wine vinegar over the chicken and season to taste. Cover and leave to marinate in the refrigerator overnight.

3 Remove the chicken pieces with a perforated spoon, draining well, and reserve the marinade.

4 Heat the oil and butter in a skillet. Add the shallots and cook for 2–3 minutes, or until they begin to soften.

5 Add the chicken pieces to the pan and cook for 3–4 minutes, turning, until browned all over. Reduce the heat and add half of the reserved marinade. Cover and cook for 15–20 minutes, adding more marinade when necessary.

6 Once the chicken is tender, add the balsamic vinegar and thyme and cook for an additional 4 minutes.

7 Transfer the chicken and marinade to serving plates and serve with polenta or rice.

cook's tip

To make the chicken pieces look a little neater, use wooden skewers to hold them together or secure them with a length of string.

shrimp-stuffed chicken on tagliatelle

These mouthwatering mini-packages of chicken and shrimp are sure to delight your guests.

Serves 4

4 tbsp butter, plus extra for greasing

4 x 7 oz chicken suprêmes, trimmed

4 oz large spinach leaves, trimmed and
    blanched in hot salted water

4 slices of prosciutto

12–16 raw jumbo shrimp, shelled and
    deveined

1 lb dried tagliatelle

1 tbsp olive oil

3 leeks, shredded

1 large carrot, grated

⅝ cup thick mayonnaise

2 large cooked beet

salt

1 Grease 4 large pieces of foil and set aside. Place each suprême between 2 pieces of baking parchment and pound with a rolling pin to flatten.

2 Divide half of the spinach between the suprêmes. Add a slice of ham to each and top with more spinach. Place 3–4 shrimp on top of the spinach. Fold the pointed end of the suprême over the shrimp, then fold over again to form a parcel. Wrap in foil, then place on a baking sheet and bake in a preheated oven at 400°F for 20 minutes.

3 Bring a pan of salted water to a boil. Add the pasta and oil and cook until tender. Drain and transfer to a large serving dish.

4 Melt the butter in a skillet. Fry the leeks and carrots for 3 minutes. Transfer the vegetables to the center of the pasta.

5 Work the mayonnaise and 1 beet in a food processor or blender until smooth. Rub through a strainer and then pour around the pasta and vegetables.

6 Cut the remaining beet into diamond shapes and place them neatly around the mayonnaise. Remove the foil from the chicken and, using a sharp knife, cut the suprêmes into thin slices. Arrange the slices on top of the vegetables and pasta, and serve.

1

2

2

duck with raspberry & honey sauce

A raspberry and honey sauce superbly counterbalances the richness of the duck.

1

3

6

Serves 4

4 x 10½ oz boned breasts of duck

2 tbsp butter

⅓ cup finely chopped carrots

4 tbsp finely chopped shallots

1 tbsp lemon juice

⅔ cup meat bouillon

4 tbsp clear honey

¾ cup fresh or thawed frozen raspberries

¼ cup all-purpose flour

1 tbsp Worcestershire sauce

14 oz fresh linguine

1 tbsp olive oil

salt and pepper

TO GARNISH

fresh raspberries

fresh sprig of flatleaf parsley

1 Trim and score the duck breasts with a sharp knife and season well all over. Melt the butter in a skillet, then add the duck breasts and cook all over until lightly colored.

2 Add the carrots, shallots, lemon juice, and half the meat bouillon and simmer over a low heat for 1 minute. Stir in half the honey and half the raspberries. Sprinkle over half the flour and cook, stirring constantly for 3 minutes. Season with pepper and add the Worcestershire sauce.

3 Stir in the remaining bouillon and cook for 1 minute. Stir in the remaining honey and remaining raspberries and sprinkle over the remaining flour. Cook for a further 3 minutes.

4 Remove the duck breasts from the pan, but leave the sauce to continue simmering over a very low heat.

5 Meanwhile, bring a large saucepan of lightly salted water to a boil. Add the linguine and olive oil and cook until tender, but still firm to the bite. Drain and divide between 4 individual plates.

6 Slice the duck breast lengthwise into ¼-inch thick pieces. Pour a little sauce over the pasta and arrange the sliced duck in a fan shape on top of it. Garnish with raspberries and flatleaf parsley and serve.

lime partridge with pesto

Partridge has a more delicate flavor than many game birds and this subtle sauce perfectly complements it.

Serves 4

8 partridge pieces (about 4 oz each)

4 tbsp butter, melted

4 tbsp Dijon mustard

2 tbsp lime juice

1 tbsp brown sugar

6 tbsp Pesto Sauce (see page 23)

1 lb dried rigatoni

1 tbsp olive oil

1⅓ cups freshly grated Parmesan cheese

salt and pepper

1 Arrange the partridge pieces, smooth-side down, in a single layer in a large, ovenproof dish.

2 Mix together the butter, Dijon mustard, lime juice, and brown sugar in a bowl. Season to taste with salt and pepper. Brush this mixture over the uppermost surfaces of the partridge pieces and bake in a preheated oven at 400°F for 15 minutes.

3 Remove the dish from the oven and coat the partridge pieces with 3 tbsp of the Pesto Sauce. Return to the oven and bake for an additional 12 minutes.

4 Remove the dish from the oven and carefully turn over the partridge pieces. Coat the top of the partridges with the remaining mustard mixture and return to the oven for an additional 10 minutes.

2

5 Meanwhile, bring a large saucepan of lightly salted water to a boil. Add the rigatoni and olive oil and cook for about 10 minutes, or until tender, but still firm to the bite. Drain and transfer to a large serving dish. Toss the pasta with the remaining Pesto Sauce and the Parmesan cheese.

6 Arrange the pieces of partridge on the serving dish with the rigatoni, then pour over the cooking juices and serve immediately.

variation

You could also prepare young pheasant in the same way.

2

3

pheasant lasagna

This scrumptious and unusual baked lasagna is virtually a meal in itself.

Serves 4

butter, for greasing

14 sheets pre-cooked lasagna

3¼ cups Béchamel Sauce

¼ cup grated mozzarella cheese

FILLING

8 oz pork fat, diced

2 tbsp butter

16 small onions

8 large pheasant breasts, thinly sliced

¼ cup all-purpose flour

2½ cups chicken bouillon

bouquet garni

1 lb fresh English peas, shelled

salt and pepper

1 To make the filling, put the pork fat into a pan of boiling, salted water and simmer for 3 minutes, then drain and pat dry.

2 Melt the butter in a large skillet. Add the pork fat and onions and cook for 3 minutes, or until lightly browned.

3 Remove the pork fat and onions from the pan and set aside. Add the slices of pheasant and cook over a low heat for 12 minutes, or until browned all over. Transfer to an ovenproof dish.

2

3

4 Stir the flour into the pan and cook until just brown, then blend in the bouillon. Pour over the pheasant and add the bouquet garni, then cook in a preheated oven at 400°F for 5 minutes.

5 Remove the bouquet garni. Add the onions, pork fat, and peas and return to the oven for 10 minutes.

6 Put the pheasant breasts and pork in a food processor and grind finely.

7 Lower the oven temperature to 375°F. Lightly grease an ovenproof dish with butter. Make layers of lasagna, ground pheasant, and Béchamel Sauce in the dish, ending with Béchamel sauce. Sprinkle over the cheese and bake in the oven for 30 minutes. Serve surrounded by the peas and onions.

6

beef in red wine with oranges & porcini

This slow-cooked beef stew is flavored with oranges, red wine, and porcini mushrooms.

Serves 4

1 tbsp oil

1 tbsp butter

8 oz baby onions, peeled and halved

1 lb 5 oz stewing steak, diced into

   1½ inch chunks

1¼ cup beef bouillon

⅔ cup red wine

4 tbsp chopped oregano

1 tbsp sugar

1 orange

1 oz porcini or other dried mushrooms

8 oz fresh plum tomatoes

cooked rice or potatoes, to serve

1 Heat the oil and butter in a large skillet. Add the onions and sauté for 5 minutes or until golden. Remove with a draining spoon, set aside and keep warm.

2 Add the beef to the pan and cook, stirring, for 5 minutes, or until browned all over.

3 Return the onions to the skillet and add the bouillon, wine, oregano, and sugar, stirring to mix well. Transfer the mixture to an ovenproof casserole dish.

2

3

4

4 Pare the peel from the orange and cut it into strips. Slice the orange flesh into rings. Add the orange rings and the peel to the casserole. Cook in a preheated oven, at 350°F, for 1¼ hours.

5 Soak the porcini mushrooms for 30 minutes in a small bowl containing 4 tablespoons of warm water.

6 Peel and halve the tomatoes. Add the tomatoes, porcini mushrooms, and their soaking liquid to the casserole. Cook for an additional 20 minutes or until the beef is tender and the juices thickened. Serve with cooked rice or potatoes.

variation

Instead of fresh tomatoes, try using 8 sun-dried tomatoes, cut into wide strips, if you prefer.

beef & pasta bake with parmesan

A recipe with both Italian and Greek origins, this dish may be served hot or cold, cut into thick satisfying squares.

Serves 4

2 cups dried fusilli

1 tbsp olive oil, plus extra for brushing

4 tbsp heavy cream

salt

fresh rosemary sprigs, to garnish

mixed salad, to serve

SAUCE

2 tbsp olive oil

1 onion, thinly sliced

1 red bell pepper, cored, seeded, and
    chopped

2 garlic cloves, chopped

5¼ cups ground beef

14 oz canned chopped tomatoes

½ cup dry white wine

2 tbsp chopped fresh parsley

2 oz canned anchovies, drained and
    chopped

salt and pepper

TOPPING

1¼ cups unsweetened yogurt

3 eggs

pinch of freshly grated nutmeg

½ cup freshly grated Parmesan cheese

1 Heat the oil in a skillet and cook the onion and red bell pepper for 3 minutes. Add the garlic and cook for 1 minute. Add the beef and cook until browned.

1

2 Add the tomatoes and wine to the pan and bring to a boil. Lower the heat and simmer for 20 minutes, or until thickened. Stir in the parsley and anchovies and season to taste.

3 Bring a pan of salted water to a boil. Add the pasta and oil and cook for 10 minutes, or until almost tender. Drain and transfer to a bowl. Stir in the cream.

4 For the topping, beat the yogurt, eggs, and nutmeg.

5 Brush an ovenproof dish with oil. Spoon in half the pasta and cover with half the meat sauce. Repeat, then spread over the topping and sprinkle with cheese.

6 Bake in a preheated oven at 375°F for 25 minutes, or until golden. Garnish with rosemary and serve with a mixed salad.

2

5

mushroom tagliarini

A different twist is given to this traditional pasta dish with a rich, but subtle, sauce.

Serves 4

2 cups white bread crumbs

⅔ cup milk

2 tbsp butter

9 tbsp olive oil

3 cups sliced oyster mushrooms

¼ cup whole-wheat flour

⅞ cup beef bouillon

⅔ cup red wine

4 tomatoes, skinned and chopped

1 tbsp tomato paste

1 tsp brown sugar

1 tbsp finely chopped fresh basil

12 shallots, chopped

4 cups ground steak

1 tsp paprika

1 lb dried egg tagliarini

salt and pepper

fresh basil sprigs, to garnish

1 Soak the bread crumbs in the milk for 30 minutes.

2 Heat half the butter and 4 tbsp of the oil in a pan. Cook the mushrooms for 4 minutes, then stir in the flour and cook for 2 minutes. Add the bouillon and wine and simmer for 15 minutes. Add the tomatoes, tomato paste, sugar, and basil. Season well and simmer for 30 minutes.

3 Mix the shallots, steak, and paprika with the bread crumbs and season. Shape the mixture into 14 meatballs.

4 Heat 4 tbsp of the remaining oil and the remaining butter in a large skillet. Fry the meatballs, turning frequently, until brown all over. Transfer to a deep casserole and pour over the red wine and the mushroom sauce. Cover and bake in a preheated oven at 350°F for 30 minutes.

5 Bring a pan of salted water to a boil. Add the pasta and the remaining oil and cook until tender. Drain and transfer to a serving dish. Remove the casserole from the oven and cool for 3 minutes. Pour the meatballs and sauce on to the pasta, then garnish with the basil sprigs and serve.

3

3

4

classic spaghetti with bolognese sauce

You can use this classic meat sauce for lasagna, cannelloni, or any other baked pasta dishes.

Serves 4

3 tbsp olive oil

2 garlic cloves, minced

1 large onion, finely chopped

1 carrot, diced

2 cups lean ground beef, veal, or chicken

3 oz chicken livers, finely chopped

3½ oz lean prosciutto, diced

⅛ cup Marsala wine

10 oz canned chopped plum tomatoes

1 tbsp chopped fresh basil leaves

2 tbsp tomato paste

salt and pepper

1 lb dried spaghetti

variation

Chicken livers are an essential ingredient in a classic Bolognese sauce to which they add richness. However, if you prefer not to use them, substitute the same quantity of ground beef.

1

2

3

1 Heat 2 tbsp of the olive oil in a large pan. Add the garlic, onion, and carrot and cook for 6 minutes.

2 Add the ground beef, veal, or chicken, chicken livers, and prosciutto to the pan and cook over a medium heat for 12 minutes, or until well browned.

3 Stir in the Marsala, tomatoes, basil, and tomato paste and cook for 4 minutes. Season. Cover and simmer for 30 minutes.

4 Remove the lid from the pan, then stir and simmer for an additional 15 minutes.

5 Meanwhile, bring a large pan of lightly salted water to a boil. Add the spaghetti and the remaining oil and cook for about 12 minutes, or until tender, but still firm to the bite. Drain and transfer to a serving dish. Pour the sauce over the pasta and toss then serve hot.

creamy beef macaroni

The combination of macaroni and beef korma gives this a really unique flavor.

Serves 4

2 lb steak, cut into cubes

⅔ cup beef bouillon

1 lb dried macaroni

1¼ cups heavy cream

½ tsp garam masala

salt

fresh cilantro, to garnish

nans, to serve

KORMA PASTE

½ cup blanched almonds

6 garlic cloves

1 inch piece fresh gingerroot,
    coarsely chopped

6 tbsp beef bouillon

1 tsp ground cardamom

4 cloves, minced

1 tsp cinnamon

2 large onions, chopped

1 tsp coriander seeds

2 tsp ground cumin seeds

pinch of cayenne pepper

6 tbsp of sunflower oil

variation

You could also make this
dish using diced chicken and
chicken bouillon, instead of
steak and beef bouillon.

1 To make the korma paste, grind the almonds finely, using a pestle and mortar. Put the ground almonds and the rest of the korma paste ingredients into a food processor or blender and process to make a very smooth paste.

2 Put the steak in a shallow dish and spoon over the korma paste, turning to coat the steak well. Let stand in the refrigerator to marinate for 6 hours.

1

2

3 Transfer the steak to a large pan, and simmer over a low heat, adding a little beef bouillon if required, for 35 minutes.

4 Meanwhile, bring a large pan of lightly salted water to a boil. Add the macaroni and cook for 10 minutes, or until tender, but still firm to the bite. Drain the pasta thoroughly and transfer to a deep casserole. Add the steak, heavy cream, and garam masala.

5 Bake in a preheated oven at 400°F for 30 minutes. Remove the casserole from the oven and let stand for about 10 minutes. Garnish the bake with fresh cilantro and serve with nans.

3

cannellini bean casserole

In this traditional Tuscan dish, Italian sausages are cooked with cannellini beans and tomatoes.

Serves 4

1 green bell pepper

8 Italian sausages

1 tbsp olive oil

1 large onion, chopped

2 garlic cloves, chopped

8 oz fresh tomatoes, skinned and chopped
    or 14 oz canned tomatoes, chopped

2 tbsp sun-dried tomato paste

14 oz canned cannellini beans

mashed potato or rice, to serve

1 Seed the bell pepper and cut it into thin strips.

2 Prick the Italian sausages all over with a fork. Cook them, under a preheated broiler, for 10–12 minutes, turning occasionally, until brown all over. Set aside and keep warm.

3 Heat the oil in a large skillet. Add the onion, garlic, and bell pepper to the skillet and cook for 5 minutes, stirring occasionally, or until softened.

4 Add the tomatoes to the skillet and let the mixture simmer for about 5 minutes, stirring occasionally, or until slightly reduced and thickened.

5 Stir the sun-dried tomato paste, cannellini beans, and Italian sausages into the mixture in the skillet. Cook for 4–5 minutes, or until the mixture is piping hot. Add 4–5 tablespoons of water, if the mixture becomes too dry during cooking.

6 Transfer the Italian sausage and bean casserole to serving plates and serve with mashed potato or rice.

cook's tip

Italian sausages are coarse in texture and have a strong flavor. They can be found in specialist sausage shops, Italian delicatessens, and some larger supermarkets. They are replaceable in this recipe only by game sausages.

3

1

5

spinach & ricotta cannelloni

It is easier to use dried pasta in this recipe—you can buy it ready-made in tubes. If you are using fresh pasta, you must cut out squares and roll them yourself.

Serves 4

20 tubes dried cannelloni (about 7 oz) or
    20 square sheets of fresh pasta (12 oz)

9 oz ricotta cheese

5½ oz frozen spinach, defrosted

½ small red bell pepper, diced

2 scallions, chopped

⅔ cup hot vegetable or chicken bouillon

1 portion of Basil and Tomato Puréed Sauce
    (see page 293)

¼ cup grated Parmesan or romano cheese

salt and pepper

variation

If you would prefer a creamier version, omit the stock and the basil and tomato puréed sauce and replace with Béchamel Sauce.

1 If you are using dried cannelloni, check the package directions; many varieties do not need pre-cooking. If necessary, pre-cook your pasta. Bring a large pan of water to a boil, add 1 tablespoon of oil, and cook the pasta for 3–4 minutes—it is easier to do this in batches.

2 In a bowl, mix together the ricotta, spinach, bell pepper, and scallions, and season to taste with salt and pepper.

3 Lightly butter an ovenproof dish large enough to contain all of the pasta tubes in a single layer. Spoon the ricotta mixture into the pasta tubes and place them into the prepared dish. If you are using fresh sheets of pasta, spread the ricotta mixture along one side of each fresh pasta square and roll up to form a tube.

4 Mix together the bouillon and basil and tomato purée and pour it all over the pasta tubes.

5 Sprinkle the cheese over the cannelloni and bake in a preheated oven, 375°F, for 20–25 minutes, or until the pasta is cooked through.

2

3

4

citrus pork chops

The addition of juniper and fennel to the pork chops gives an unusual and delicate flavor to this dish.

1

2

5

Serves 4

½ fennel bulb

1 tbsp juniper berries, lightly crushed

about 2 tbsp olive oil

finely grated rind and juice of 1 orange

4 pork chops, each about 5½ oz

fresh bread and a crisp salad, to serve

1 Using a sharp knife, finely chop the fennel bulb, discarding the leaves and green parts.

2 Grind the juniper berries in a mortar and pestle. Mix the minced juniper berries with the fennel flesh, olive oil, and orange peel.

3 Using a sharp knife, score a few cuts all over each chop.

4 Place the pork chops in a roasting pan or an ovenproof dish. Spoon the fennel and juniper mixture over each of the pork chops.

5 Carefully pour the orange juice over the top of each pork chop. Cover, and let marinate in the refrigerator for about 2 hours.

6 Cook the pork chops, under a preheated broiler, for 10–15 minutes, depending on the thickness of the meat, until the meat is tender and cooked through, turning occasionally.

7 Transfer the pork chops to serving plates and serve with a crisp, fresh salad and plenty of fresh bread to mop up the cooking juices.

cook's tip

Juniper berries are most commonly associated with gin, but they are often added to meat dishes in Italy for a delicate citrus flavor. They can be bought dried from most health-food shops and some larger supermarkets.

pork pockets with almonds & prosciutto

This is a simplified version of a traditional dish from the Marche region, on the east coast of Italy. Pork fillet pockets are stuffed with prosciutto and herbs.

Serves 4

1 lb pork fillet

1¼ oz chopped almonds

2 tbsp olive oil

3½ oz prosciutto, finely chopped

2 garlic cloves, chopped

1 tbsp fresh oregano, chopped

finely grated peel of 2 lemons

4 shallots, finely chopped

¾ cup ham or chicken bouillon

1 tsp sugar

4

4

1

1 Using a sharp knife, cut the pork fillet into 4 equal pieces. Place the pork between sheets of oiled paper and pound each piece with a meat mallet or the end of a rolling pin to flatten it.

2 Cut a horizontal slit in each piece of pork to make a pocket.

3 Place the almonds on a baking sheet. Lightly toast the almonds under a medium-hot broiler for 2–3 minutes, or until golden.

4 Mix the almonds with 1 tablespoon of the olive oil, chopped prosciutto, garlic, oregano, and the finely grated peel from 1 lemon. Spoon the mixture into the pockets of the pork.

5 Heat the remaining oil in a large skillet. Add the shallots and cook for 2 minutes.

6 Add the pork to the skillet and cook for 2 minutes on each side, or until browned all over.

7 Add the bouillon to the pan and bring to a boil. Cover and let simmer for 45 minutes, or until the pork is tender. Remove the meat from the pan, then set aside and keep warm.

8 Using a zester, pare the remaining lemon. Add the peel and sugar to the pan, then boil for 3–4 minutes, or until reduced and syrupy. Pour over the pork fillets and serve immediately.

veal, mushroom & mascarpone pasta

The delicious combination of apple, onion, and mushroom perfectly complements the delicate flavor of veal.

Serves 4

⅓ cup butter

4 x 9 oz veal cutlets, trimmed

1 large onion, sliced

2 apples, peeled, cored, and sliced

6 oz white mushrooms

1 tbsp chopped fresh tarragon

8 black peppercorns

1 tbsp sesame seeds

14 oz dried marille

scant ½ cup extra-virgin olive oil

¾ cup mascarpone cheese, broken into small pieces

salt and pepper

2 large beefsteak tomatoes, cut in half

leaves of 1 fresh basil sprig

fresh basil leaves, to garnish

1 Melt 4 tbsp of the butter in a skillet. Cook the veal over a low heat for 5 minutes on each side. Transfer to a dish and keep warm.

2 Cook the onion and apples in the skillet until lightly browned. Transfer to a dish, then place the veal on top and keep warm.

3 Melt the remaining butter in the skillet. Gently cook the mushrooms, tarragon, and peppercorns over a low heat for 3 minutes. Sprinkle over the sesame seeds.

4 Bring a pan of salted water to a boil. Add the pasta and 1 tbsp of the oil. Cook until tender, but still firm to the bite. Drain and transfer to a serving plate.

5 Top the pasta with the mascarpone and sprinkle over the remaining olive oil. Place the onions, apples, and veal cutlets on top of the pasta. Spoon the mushrooms and peppercorns on to the cutlets, then place the tomatoes and basil leaves around the edge. Place in a preheated oven at 300°F for 5 minutes.

6 Season to taste with salt and pepper, then garnish with fresh basil leaves, and serve immediately.

1

2

3

Pasta is a natural partner for fish and seafood. Both are cooked quickly to preserve their flavor and texture, they are packed full of nutritional goodness, and the varieties available are almost infinite. These recipes feature exciting and tempting ways of cooking fish and meat to make a range of satisfying meals that are typically Italian. Fish is one of the most important food sources in Italy. The fish markets there are fascinating, with a huge variety of local fish on display. Fresh or frozen imported fish of all kinds from the Mediterranean are appearing increasingly in fishmongers and supermarkets, giving us access to dishes that were once only the preserve of the Italians. This chapter contains a wealth of fish and seafood recipes to suit all occasions.

fish &
shellfish

tuna pasta with parsley sauce

The classic Italian combination of pasta and tuna is enhanced in this recipe with a delicious parsley sauce.

Serves 4

7 oz canned tuna, drained

2 oz canned anchovies, drained

1¼ cups olive oil

1 cup coarsely chopped flatleaf parsley

¾ cup crème fraîche

1 lb dried spaghetti

2 tbsp butter

salt and pepper

black olives, to garnish

crusty bread, to serve

1 Remove any bones from the tuna. Put the tuna into a food processor or blender, together with the anchovies, 1 cup olive oil, and the flatleaf parsley. Process until the sauce is smooth.

2 Spoon the crème fraîche into the food processor or blender and process again for a few seconds to blend thoroughly. Season to taste with salt and black pepper.

3 Bring a large pan of lightly salted water to a boil. Add the spaghetti and the remaining olive oil and cook until tender, but still firm to the bite.

4 Drain the spaghetti, then return to the pan and place over a medium heat. Add the butter and toss well to coat. Spoon in the sauce and quickly toss into the spaghetti, using 2 forks.

5 Remove the pan from the heat and divide the spaghetti between 4 warm individual serving plates. Garnish with the olives and serve immediately with warm, crusty bread.

2

variation

For a change, add 1-2 garlic cloves to the sauce, substitute ½ cup chopped fresh basil for half the parsley, and garnish with capers instead of black olives.

4

4

herb-roasted cod with lemon & rosemary

Cod roasted with herbs and topped with a lemon and rosemary crust is a delicious main course.

Serves 4

2 tbsp butter

⅓ cup whole-wheat bread crumbs

1 oz chopped walnuts

grated peel and juice of 2 lemons

2 sprigs rosemary, stalks removed

2 tbsp chopped parsley

4 cod fillets, each about 5¼ oz

1 garlic clove, minced

1 small red chile, diced

3 tbsp walnut oil

salad leaves, to serve

variation

If preferred, the walnuts may be omitted from the crust. In addition, extra-virgin olive oil can be used instead of walnut oil, if you prefer.

1 Melt the butter in a large skillet.

2 Remove the skillet from the heat and add the bread crumbs, walnuts, the peel and juice of 1 lemon, half of the rosemary, and half of the parsley.

3 Press the bread crumb mixture over the top of the cod fillets. Place the fillets in a shallow, foil-lined roasting pan.

cook's tip

The hotness of chiles varies so use them with caution. As a general guide, the smaller the chile, the hotter it will be.

4 Bake in a preheated oven at 400°F for 25–30 minutes.

5 Mix the garlic, the remaining lemon peel and juice, rosemary, parsley, and chile in a bowl. Beat in the walnut oil and mix to combine well. Drizzle the dressing over the cod steaks as soon as they are cooked.

6 Transfer to serving plates and serve immediately.

2

2

3

salt cod cakes with fennel

These tasty fried cakes of mashed salt cod mixed with fennel and chile make an excellent snack or main course served with vegetables and a chile relish.

Serves 4

scant ⅔ cup self-rising flour

1 egg, beaten

⅔ cup milk

9 oz salt cod, soaked overnight

1 small red onion, finely chopped

1 small fennel bulb, finely chopped

1 red chile, finely chopped

2 tbsp oil

TO SERVE

crisp salad, chile relish, cooked rice, and
    fresh vegetables

1 Sift the flour into a large bowl. Make a well in the center of the flour and add the egg.

2 Using a wooden spoon, gradually draw in the flour, slowly adding the milk, and mix to form a smooth batter. Leave to stand for 10 minutes.

3 Drain the salt cod and rinse it under cold running water. Drain again thoroughly.

4 Remove and discard the skin and any bones from the fish, then mash the flesh with a fork.

5 Place the fish in a large bowl and combine with the onion, fennel, and chile. Add the mixture to the batter and blend together.

6 Heat the oil in a large skillet and, taking about 1 tablespoon of the mixture at a time, spoon it into the hot oil. Cook the fritters, in batches, for 3–4 minutes on each side, until golden and slightly puffed. Keep warm while cooking the remaining mixture.

7 Serve with salad and a chile relish for a light meal or with vegetables and rice for a main course.

cook's tip

If you prefer larger fritters, use 2 tablespoons per fritter and cook for slightly longer.

2

5

5

cod with tomatoes & tarragon

Salt cod is dried and salted in order to preserve it. It has an unusual flavor, which goes particularly well with celery in this dish.

Serves 4

9 oz salt cod, soaked overnight

1 tbsp oil

4 shallots, finely chopped

2 garlic cloves, chopped

3 celery stalks, chopped

14 oz canned tomatoes, chopped

⅔ cup fish bouillon

1¾ oz pine nuts

2 tbsp coarsely chopped tarragon

2 tbsp capers

crusty bread or mashed potato, to serve

1 Drain the salt cod. Rinse it under plenty of running water and drain again thoroughly. Remove and discard any skin and bones. Pat the fish dry with paper towels and cut it into chunks.

2 Heat the oil in a large skillet. Add the shallots and garlic and cook for 2–3 minutes. Add the celery and cook for an additional 2 minutes, then add the tomatoes and bouillon.

3 Bring the mixture to a boil, then reduce the heat and let simmer for 5 minutes.

1

2

5

4 Add the fish and cook for 10 minutes, or until tender.

5 Meanwhile, place the pine nuts on a cookie sheet. Place under a preheated broiler and toast for about 2–3 minutes, or until golden.

6 Stir the tarragon, capers, and pine nuts into the fish casserole and heat gently to warm through.

7 Transfer to serving plates and serve at once with fresh crusty bread or mashed potato.

cook's tip

Salt cod is a useful ingredient to keep in the pantry and, once soaked, can be used in the same way as any other fish. It does, however, have a stronger flavor than normal, and it is slightly salty. It can be found in fishmongers, larger supermarkets, and delicatessens.

smoked salmon pasta with whiskey sauce

Made in moments, this is a luxurious dish to astonish and delight unexpected guests.

Serves 4

1 lb dried buckwheat spaghetti

2 tbsp olive oil

½ cup crumbled feta cheese

salt

fresh cilantro or parsley leaves, to garnish

SAUCE

1¼ cups heavy cream

⅔ cup whiskey or brandy

4½ oz smoked salmon

pinch of cayenne pepper

black pepper

2 tbsp chopped fresh cilantro or parsley

1 Bring a large pan of lightly salted water to a boil. Add the spaghetti and 1 tbsp of the olive oil and cook until tender, but still firm to the bite. Drain the spaghetti, then return to the pan and sprinkle over the remaining olive oil. Cover and shake the pan, then set aside and keep warm.

2 Pour the cream into a small pan and bring to simmering point, but do not let it boil. Pour the whiskey or brandy into another small pan and bring to simmering point, but do not let it boil. Remove both pans from the heat and mix together the cream and whiskey or brandy.

2

3

3

3 Cut the smoked salmon into thin strips and add to the cream mixture. Season to taste with cayenne and black pepper. Just before serving, stir in the chopped fresh cilantro or parsley.

4 Transfer the spaghetti to a warm serving dish, then pour over the sauce and toss thoroughly with 2 large forks. Scatter over the crumbled feta cheese and garnish with the cilantro or parsley leaves. Serve immediately.

red mullet medallions with creamy lemon sauce

A favorite fish for chefs, the delicious red mullet is now becoming increasingly common in supermarkets and fish stores for family meals.

Serves 4

1 lb dried macaroni

1 tbsp olive oil

8 x 4 oz red mullet medallions

TO GARNISH
lemon slices
shredded leek
shredded carrot

SAUCE
2 tbsp butter
4 shallots, chopped
2 tbsp capers
1½ cups pitted green olives, chopped
4 tbsp balsamic vinegar
1¼ cups fish bouillon
1¼ cups heavy cream
juice of 1 lemon
salt and pepper

1 To make the sauce, melt the butter in a skillet. Add the shallots and cook over a low heat for 4 minutes. Add the capers and olives and cook for an additional 3 minutes.

2 Stir in the balsamic vinegar and fish bouillon, then bring to a boil and reduce by half. Add the cream, stirring, and reduce again by half. Season to taste with salt and pepper and stir in the lemon juice. Remove the pan from the heat, then set aside and keep warm.

3 Bring a large saucepan of lightly salted water to a boil. Add the pasta and olive oil and cook for about 12 minutes, until tender but still firm to the bite.

4 Meanwhile, lightly broil the red mullet medallions for 3–4 minutes on each side, until cooked through, but still moist.

5 Drain the pasta thoroughly and transfer to large individual serving dishes. Top the pasta with the fish medallions and pour over the olive sauce. Garnish with lemon slices, shredded leek, and shredded carrot, and serve immediately.

1

2

2

macaroni pudding

A tasty mixture of creamy fish and pasta cooked in a bowl, then unmolded and drizzled with tomato sauce presents macaroni in a new guise.

2

3

3

Serves 4

1 cup dried short-cut macaroni or other
  short pasta

1 tbsp olive oil

1 tbsp butter, plus extra for oiling

1 lb white fish fillets, such as cod
  or haddock

2–3 fresh parsley sprigs

6 black peppercorns

½ cup heavy cream

2 eggs, separated

2 tbsp chopped fresh dill or parsley

pinch of freshly grated nutmeg

⅔ cup freshly grated Parmesan cheese

salt and pepper

fresh dill or parsley sprigs, to garnish

tomato sauce to serve

1 Bring a pan of salted water to a boil. Add the pasta and olive oil and cook until tender, but still firm to the bite. Drain the pasta, then return to the pan and add the butter. Cover, and keep warm.

2 Place the fish in a skillet. Add the parsley sprigs, peppercorns, and enough water to cover. Bring to a boil, then cover and simmer for 10 minutes. Lift out the fish and set aside to cool. Reserve the cooking liquid.

3 Skin the fish and cut into bite-size pieces. Put the pasta in a bowl. Mix the cream, egg yolks, chopped dill or parsley, nutmeg, and cheese, then pour into the pasta and mix. Spoon in the fish without breaking it. Add enough of the reserved cooking liquid to make a moist, but firm mixture. Whisk the egg whites until stiff, then fold them into the mixture.

4 Grease a heatproof bowl and spoon in the fish mixture to within 1½ inches of the rim. Cover with greased baking parchment and foil and tie with string.

5 Stand the bowl on a trivet in a pan. Add boiling water to reach halfway up the sides. Cover and steam for 1½ hours.

6 Invert the pudding on to a serving plate. Pour over a little tomato sauce. Garnish and serve with the remaining tomato sauce.

red mullet with golden raisins & orange

Red mullet has a beautiful pink skin, which is enhanced in this dish by being cooked in red wine and orange juice.

Serves 4

1¾ oz golden raisins

⅔ cup red wine

2 tbsp olive oil

2 medium onions, sliced

1 zucchini cut into 2 inch sticks

2 oranges

2 tsp coriander seeds, lightly ground

4 red mullet, boned and filleted

1¾ oz canned anchovy fillets, drained

2 tbsp chopped, fresh oregano

4

5

1 Place the golden raisins in a bowl. Pour over the red wine and let soak for 10 minutes.

2 Heat the oil in a large skillet. Add the onions and sauté for 2 minutes.

3

3 Add the zucchini and cook for 3 minutes, or until tender.

4 Using a zester, pare long, thin strips from one of the oranges. Using a sharp knife, remove the skin from both of the oranges, then segment the oranges by slicing between the lines of pith.

5 Add the orange zest to the skillet. Add the red wine, golden raisins, red mullet, and anchovies to the pan and let simmer for 10–15 minutes, or until the fish is cooked through.

6 Stir in the oregano, then set aside and cool. Place the mixture in a large bowl and let chill, covered, in the refrigerator for at least 2 hours to let the flavors mingle. Transfer to serving plates and serve.

red mullet with almond liqueur

This succulent fish and pasta dish is ideal for serving on a warm, summer's evening—preferably al fresco.

Serves 4

3¾ cups all-purpose flour

8 red mullet fillets

2 tbsp butter

⅔ cup fish bouillon

1 tbsp crushed almonds

1 tsp pink peppercorns

1 orange, peeled and cut into segments

1 tbsp orange liqueur

grated peel of 1 orange

1 lb dried orecchiette

1 tbsp olive oil

⅔ cup heavy cream

4 tbsp amaretto

salt and pepper

TO GARNISH

2 tbsp snipped fresh chives

1 tbsp toasted almonds

2

3

1

1 Season the flour with salt and pepper and sprinkle into a shallow bowl. Press the fish fillets into the flour to coat. Melt the butter in a skillet. Add the fish and cook over a low heat for about 3 minutes, or until browned.

2 Add the fish bouillon to the pan and cook for 4 minutes. Carefully remove the fish, then cover with foil and keep warm.

3 Add the almonds, pink peppercorns, half the orange, the orange liqueur, and orange peel to the pan. Simmer until the liquid has reduced by half.

4 Meanwhile, bring a large pan of lightly salted water to a boil. Add the orecchiette and olive oil and cook for 15 minutes, or until tender, but still firm to the bite.

5 Meanwhile, season the sauce with salt and pepper and stir in the cream and amaretto. Cook for 2 minutes. Return the fish to the pan to coat with the sauce.

6 Drain the pasta and transfer to a serving dish. Top with the fish fillets and their sauce. Garnish with the remaining orange segments, the chives, and toasted almonds. Serve immediately.

salmon in lemon & watercress sauce

Fresh salmon and pasta in a mouthwatering lemon and watercress sauce—
a wonderful summer evening treat.

Serves 4

4 x 10 oz fresh salmon steaks

4 tbsp butter

¼ cup dry white wine

sea salt

8 peppercorns

fresh dill sprig

fresh tarragon sprig

1 lemon, sliced

1 lb dried penne

2 tbsp olive oil

lemon slices and fresh watercress,
    to garnish

LEMON & WATERCRESS SAUCE

2 tbsp butter

¼ cup all-purpose flour

⅔ cup warm milk

juice and finely grated peel of
    2 lemons

2 oz watercress, chopped

salt and pepper

1 Put the salmon in a large, non-stick pan. Add the butter, wine, a pinch of sea salt, the peppercorns, dill, tarragon, and lemon. Cover and bring to a boil, then simmer for 10 minutes.

2 Using a slice, carefully remove the salmon. Strain and reserve the cooking liquid. Remove and discard the salmon skin and center bones. Place on a warm dish, then cover and keep warm.

1

3 Meanwhile, bring a pan of salted water to a boil. Add the penne and 1 tbsp of the oil and cook for 12 minutes, or until tender, but still firm to the bite. Drain and sprinkle over the remaining olive oil. Place on a warm serving dish and top with the salmon steaks, then keep warm.

4 To make the sauce, melt the butter and stir in the flour for 2 minutes. Stir in the milk and about 7 tbsp of the reserved cooking liquid. Add the lemon juice and peel and cook, stirring, for an additional 10 minutes.

5 Add the watercress to the sauce and stir gently, then season to taste with salt and pepper.

6 Pour the sauce over the salmon and penne, then garnish with slices of lemon and fresh watercress. Serve immediately.

4

5

smoked haddock & lemon casserole

This quick, easy, and inexpensive dish would be ideal for a mid-week family supper.

Serves 4

2 tbsp butter, plus extra for oiling

1 lb smoked haddock fillets, cut into 4 slices

2¼ cups milk

¼ cup all-purpose flour

pinch of freshly grated nutmeg

3 tbsp heavy cream

1 tbsp chopped fresh parsley

2 eggs, hard-cooked and mashed to a pulp

4 cups dried fusilli

1 tbsp lemon juice

salt and pepper

boiled new potatoes and beet, to serve

1 Thoroughly grease a casserole with butter. Put the haddock in the casserole and pour over the milk. Bake in a preheated oven at 400°F for about 15 minutes. Carefully pour the cooking liquid into a pitcher without breaking up the fish.

2 Melt the butter in a pan and stir in the flour. Gradually whisk in the reserved cooking liquid. Season to taste with salt, pepper, and nutmeg. Stir in the cream, parsley, and mashed egg and cook, stirring constantly, for 2 minutes.

3 Meanwhile, bring a large saucepan of lightly salted water to a boil. Add the fusilli and lemon juice and cook until tender, but still firm to the bite.

4 Drain the pasta and spoon or tip it over the fish. Top with the sauce and return the casserole to the oven for 10 minutes.

5 Serve the casserole with boiled new potatoes and beet.

variation

You can use any type of dried pasta for this casserole. Try penne, conchiglie, or rigatoni.

2

1

4

bacon-wrapped trout with apple & mint

Most trout available nowadays is farmed rainbow trout. However, if you can, buy wild brown trout for this recipe.

Serves 4

butter, for greasing

4 x 9¼ oz trout, gutted and cleaned

12 anchovies in oil, drained and chopped

2 apples, peeled, cored, and sliced

4 fresh mint sprigs

juice of 1 lemon

12 strips rindless smoked fatty bacon

1 lb dried tagliatelle

1 tbsp olive oil

salt and pepper

TO GARNISH

2 apples, cored and sliced

4 fresh mint sprigs

3

3

1 Grease a deep cookie sheet thoroughly with butter.

2 Open up the cavities of each trout and wash them thoroughly with warm salt water.

3 Season each cavity with salt and black pepper. Divide the anchovies, sliced apples, and mint sprigs between each of the cavities. Sprinkle the lemon juice into each cavity.

4 Carefully cover the whole of each trout, except the head and tail, with three slices of smoked bacon in a spiral.

5 Arrange the trout on the cookie sheet with the loose ends of bacon tucked underneath. Season with black pepper and bake in a preheated oven at 400°F for 20 minutes, turning the trout over after 10 minutes.

6 Meanwhile, bring a large pan of lightly salted water to a boil. Add the tagliatelle and olive oil and cook for about 12 minutes, or until tender, but still firm to the bite. Drain the pasta and transfer to a large, warm serving dish.

7 Remove the trout from the oven and arrange on the tagliatelle. Garnish with sliced apples and fresh mint sprigs and serve immediately.

4

citrus mackerel stuffed with almonds & olives

Mackerel can be quite rich, but when it is stuffed with oranges and toasted ground almonds it is tangy and light.

Serves 4

2 tbsp oil

4 scallions, chopped

2 oranges

1¼ oz ground almonds

1 tbsp oats

1¼ oz mixed green and black olives, pitted and chopped

8 mackerel fillets

salt and pepper

crisp salad, to serve

1 Heat the oil in a skillet. Add the scallions and cook for about 2 minutes.

2 Finely grate the peel of the oranges, then, using a sharp knife, cut away the remaining skin and white pith.

3 Using a sharp knife, segment the oranges by cutting down either side of the lines of pith to loosen each segment. Do this over a plate so that you can reserve any juices. Cut each orange segment in half.

4 Lightly toast the almonds, under a preheated broiler, for 2–3 minutes, or until golden; watch them as they will brown quickly.

5 Mix the scallions, oranges, ground almonds, oats, and olives together in a bowl and season with salt and pepper.

6 Spoon the orange mixture along the center of each fillet. Roll up each fillet, securing it in place with a toothpick or skewer.

7 Bake in a preheated oven at 375°F for 25 minutes, or until the fish is tender.

8 Transfer to serving plates and serve warm with a salad.

1

5

6

sardine & vegetable bake

Here, fresh sardines are baked with eggs, herbs, and vegetables to form a dish similar to an omelet.

Serves 4

2 tbsp olive oil

2 large onions, sliced into rings

3 garlic cloves, chopped

2 large zucchini, cut into sticks

3 tbsp fresh thyme, stalks removed

8 sardine fillets or about 2 lb 4 oz
   whole sardines, filleted

¾ cup grated Parmesan cheese

4 eggs, beaten

⅔ pint milk

salt and pepper

1 Heat 1 tablespoon of the oil in a skillet. Add the onions and garlic and sauté for 2–3 minutes.

2 Add the zucchini sticks to the skillet and cook for about 5 minutes or until golden.

3 Stir 2 tablespoons of the thyme into the mixture.

4 Place half of the onions and zucchini in the base of a large ovenproof dish. Top with the sardine fillets and half of the Parmesan cheese.

2

4

4

5 Place the remaining onions and zucchini on top and sprinkle with the remaining thyme.

6 Mix the eggs and milk together in a bowl and season to taste with salt and pepper. Pour the mixture over the vegetables and sardines in the dish. Sprinkle the remaining Parmesan cheese over the top.

7 Bake in a preheated oven at 350°F for 20–25 minutes, or until golden and set. Serve hot, straight from the oven.

variation

If you cannot find sardines that are large enough to fillet, use small mackerel instead.

broiled herrings with anchovy pesto

By making a simple pesto sauce, but omitting the cheese, it is possible to heat the paste without it becoming stringy, so it can be used as a hot sauce.

3

4

5

Serves 4

4 whole herrings or small mackerel, cleaned and gutted

2 tbsp olive oil

8 oz tomatoes, peeled, deseeded, and chopped

8 canned anchovy fillets, chopped

about 30 fresh basil leaves

1¾ oz pine nuts

2 garlic cloves, minced

 1 Cook the herrings under a preheated broiler for about 8–10 minutes on each side, or until the skin is slightly charred on both sides.

2 Meanwhile, heat 1 tablespoon of the olive oil in a pan.

3 Add the tomatoes and anchovies to the pan and cook over a medium heat for 5 minutes.

4 Meanwhile, place the basil, pine nuts, garlic, and remaining oil into a food processor and blend to form a smooth paste. Alternatively, pound the ingredients by hand in a mortar and pestle.

5 Add the pesto mixture to the pan containing the tomato and anchovy mixture, and stir to heat through.

6 Spoon some of the pesto sauce on to warm individual serving plates. Place the fish on top and pour the rest of the pesto sauce over the fish. Serve immediately.

cook's tip

Try grilling the fish for an extra char-grilled flavor, if you prefer.

mixed seafood & leek lasagna

This is one of those recipes where you can use any fish and any sauce you like: from smoked finnan haddock with a little whiskey sauce to cod with cheese sauce.

Serves 4

1 lb finnan haddock, filleted, skin removed, and flesh flaked

4 oz shrimp

4 oz sole fillet, skin removed and flesh sliced

juice of 1 lemon

4 tbsp butter

3 leeks, very thinly sliced

½ cup all-purpose flour

2⅓ cups milk

2 tbsp honey

1¾ cups grated mozzarella cheese

1 lb pre-cooked lasagna

⅔ cup freshly grated Parmesan cheese

black pepper

1

3

3

1 Put the haddock fillet, shrimp, and sole fillet into a large bowl and season with black pepper and lemon juice. Set aside while you start to make the sauce.

2 Melt the butter in a large saucepan. Add the leeks and cook, stirring occasionally, for 8 minutes. Add the flour and cook, stirring constantly, for 1 minute. Gradually stir in enough milk to make a thick, creamy sauce.

3 Blend in the honey and mozzarella cheese and cook for an additional 3 minutes. Remove the pan from the heat and mix in the fish and shrimp.

4 Make alternate layers of fish sauce and lasagna in an ovenproof dish, finishing with a layer of fish sauce on top. Generously sprinkle over the grated Parmesan cheese and bake in a preheated oven at 350°F for 30 minutes. Serve immediately.

variation

For a cider sauce, substitute 1 finely chopped shallot for the leeks, 1¼ cups cider, and 1¼ cups heavy cream for the milk, and 1 tsp mustard for the honey.

For a Tuscan sauce, substitute 1 finely chopped fennel bulb for the leeks and omit the honey.

baked seafood & macaroni with fennel

This adaptation of an eighteenth-century Italian dish is baked until it is golden brown and sizzling, then cut into wedges like a cake.

Serves 4

3 cups dried short-cut macaroni

1 tbsp olive oil, plus extra for brushing

6 tbsp butter, plus extra for greasing

2 small fennel bulbs, thinly sliced and
   fronds reserved

6 oz mushrooms, thinly sliced

6 oz peeled, cooked shrimp

pinch of cayenne pepper

1¼ cups Béchamel Sauce (see Cook's Tip)

½ cup freshly grated Parmesan cheese

2 large tomatoes, sliced

1 tsp dried oregano

salt and pepper

1 Bring a pan of salted water to a boil. Add the pasta and oil and cook until tender, but still firm to the bite. Drain and return to the pan. Add 2 tbsp of butter, then cover and shake the pan. Keep warm.

2 Melt the remaining butter in a pan. Fry the fennel for 3–4 minutes. Stir in the mushrooms and cook for an additional 2 minutes. Stir in the shrimp, then remove the pan from the heat.

3 Stir the cayenne pepper and shrimp mixture into the Béchamel sauce. Pour into a greased ovenproof dish and spread evenly. Sprinkle over the Parmesan cheese and arrange the tomato slices in a ring around the edge. Brush the tomatoes with olive oil and sprinkle over the oregano.

4 Bake in a preheated oven at 350°F for 25 minutes, until golden brown. Serve immediately.

cook's tip

For Béchamel sauce, melt 2 tbsp butter. Stir in ¼ cup flour. Cook, stirring, for 2 minutes. Gradually, stir in 1¼ cups warm milk. Add 2 tbsp finely chopped onion, 5 white peppercorns, and 2 parsley sprigs, then season with salt, dried thyme, and grated nutmeg. Simmer, stirring, for 15 minutes. Strain before using.

2

2

3

mixed fish ravioli

This delicate-tasting dish is surprisingly satisfying for even the hungriest appetites.

Serves 4

12 scallops

3 tbsp olive oil

3 cups small, dried whole-wheat pasta shells

⅔ cup fish bouillon

1 onion, chopped

juice and finely grated peel of 2 lemons

⅔ cup heavy cream

2 cups grated hard cheese

salt and pepper

crusty brown bread, to serve

1 Remove the scallops from their shells. Scrape off the skirt and the black intestinal thread. Reserve the white part (the flesh) and the orange part (the coral or roe). Very carefully ease the flesh and coral from the shell with a short, but very strong knife.

2 Wash the shells thoroughly and dry them well. Put the shells on a cookie sheet. Sprinkle lightly with about two-thirds of the olive oil and set aside.

3 Meanwhile, bring a large pan of lightly salted water to a boil. Add the pasta shells and remaining olive oil and cook for about 12 minutes, or until tender, but still firm to the bite. Drain and spoon about 1 oz of pasta into each scallop shell.

4 Put the scallops, fish bouillon and onion in an ovenproof dish and season to taste with pepper. Cover with foil and bake in a preheated oven at 350°F for 8 minutes.

5 Remove the dish from the oven. Remove the foil and, using a draining spoon, transfer the scallops to the shells. Add 1 tbsp of the cooking liquid to each shell, together with a drizzle of lemon juice and a little cream, then top with the grated cheese.

6 Increase the oven temperature to 450°F and return the scallops to the oven for an additional 4 minutes.

7 Serve the scallops in their shells with crusty brown bread and butter.

4

5

5

pasta with clams & white wine

Fresh clams are available from most good fishmongers. If you prefer, used canned clams, which are less messy to eat but not so pretty to serve.

3

4

5 Meanwhile, cook the pasta in a saucepan of boiling water according to the instructions on the packet, or until it is cooked through, but still has bite. Drain.

6 Stir the tarragon into the sauce and season to taste.

7 Transfer the pasta to a serving plate and pour over the sauce.

Serves 4

1 lb 8 oz fresh clams or 10 oz canned
    clams, drained

2 tbsp olive oil

2 cloves garlic, finely chopped

14 oz mixed seafood, such as shrimps,
    squid, and mussels, defrosted if frozen

⅔ cup white wine

⅔ cup fish bouillon

2 tbsp chopped tarragon

salt and pepper

1 lb 8 oz fresh pasta or 12 oz dried pasta

1 If you are using fresh clams, scrub them clean and discard any that are already open.

2 Heat the oil in a large skillet. Add the garlic and the clams to the pan and cook for 2 minutes, shaking the pan to ensure that all of the clams are coated in the oil.

3 Add the remaining seafood mixture to the pan and cook for an additional 2 minutes.

4 Pour the wine and bouillon over the mixed seafood and garlic and bring to a boil. Cover the pan, then reduce the heat and let simmer for 8–10 minutes or until the shells open. Discard any clams or mussels that do not open.

6

variation

Red clam sauce can be made by adding 8 tablespoons of tomato paste to the sauce along with the bouillon in step 4. Follow the same cooking method.

seafood risotto with oregano

This Genoese risotto is cooked in a different way from any of the other risottos. First, you cook the rice, then you prepare a sauce, then you mix the two together. The results are just as delicious though!

Serves 4

5 cups hot fish or chicken bouillon

12 oz risotto rice, washed

3 tbsp butter

2 garlic cloves, chopped

9 oz mixed seafood, preferably raw, such as shrimp, squid, mussels, clams, and small shrimp

2 tbsp chopped oregano, plus extra for garnishing

½ cup romano or grated Parmesan cheese

1 In a large pan, bring the bouillon to a boil. Add the rice and cook for about 12 minutes, stirring, until the rice is tender, or according to the instructions on the packet. Drain thoroughly, reserving any excess liquid.

2 Heat the butter in a large skillet and add the garlic, stirring.

3 Add the raw mixed seafood to the skillet and cook for 5 minutes. If the seafood is already cooked, fry for about 2–3 minutes.

4 Stir the oregano into the seafood mixture in the skillet.

5 Add the cooked rice to the pan and cook for 2–3 minutes, stirring, until hot. Add the reserved bouillon if the mixture gets too sticky.

6 Add the pecorino or Parmesan cheese and mix well.

7 Transfer the risotto to warm serving dishes and serve immediately.

1

3

5

cook's tip

The Genoese are excellent cooks, and they make particularly delicious fish dishes flavored with the local olive oil.

spicy mussels in wine

Mussels are not difficult to cook, just a little messy to eat. The flavors are worth it, however, and serving this dish with a finger bowl helps to keep things clean!

Serves 4

2 lb 4 oz mussels

⅔ cup white wine

1 tbsp oil

1 onion, finely chopped

3 garlic cloves, chopped

1 red chile, finely chopped

3½ oz tomato paste

1 tbsp chopped marjoram

toast or crusty bread, to serve

1 Scrub the mussels to remove any mud or sand.

2 Remove the beards from the mussels by pulling away the hairy bit between the two shells. Rinse the mussels in a bowl of clean water. Discard any mussels that do not close when they are tapped— they are dead and should not be eaten.

3 Place the mussels in a large pan. Pour in the wine and cook for 5 minutes, shaking the pan occasionally until the shells open. Remove and discard any mussels that do not open.

4 Remove the mussels from the pan with a perforated spoon. Strain the cooking liquid through a fine strainer set over a bowl, then reserve the liquid.

5 Heat the oil in a large skillet. Add the onion, garlic, and chile and cook for 4–5 minutes, or until softened.

6 Add the reserved cooking liquid to the pan and cook for 5 minutes, or until reduced.

7 Stir in the tomato paste, marjoram, and mussels and cook until hot.

4

8 Transfer to serving bowls and serve with toast or plenty of crusty bread to mop up the juices.

2

3

cook's tip

Finger bowls are individual bowls of warm water with a slice of lemon floating in them. They are used to clean your fingers at the end of a meal.

clam & wine pasta with mixed herbs

A quickly cooked recipe that transforms pantry ingredients into a dish with style.

Serves 4

14 oz dried vermicelli, spaghetti or other
    long pasta

2 tbsp olive oil

2 tbsp butter

2 onions, chopped

2 garlic cloves, chopped

2 x 7 oz jars clams in brine

⅓ cup white wine

4 tbsp chopped fresh parsley

½ tsp dried oregano

pinch of freshly grated nutmeg

salt and pepper

TO GARNISH

2 tbsp Parmesan cheese shavings

fresh basil sprigs

1 Bring a large pan of lightly salted water to a boil. Add the pasta and half the olive oil and cook until tender, but still firm to the bite. Drain, then return to the pan and add the butter. Cover the pan and shake well. Keep warm.

2

2 Heat the remaining oil in a pan over a medium heat. Add the onions and cook until they are translucent. Stir in the garlic and cook for 1 minute.

3 Strain the liquid from 1 jar of clams and add the liquid to the pan, with the wine. Stir, then bring to simmering point and simmer for 3 minutes. Drain the second jar of clams and discard the liquid.

4 Add the clams, parsley, and oregano to the pan and season with pepper and nutmeg. Lower the heat and cook until the sauce is heated through.

5 Transfer the pasta to a warm serving dish and pour over the sauce. Sprinkle with the Parmesan cheese and garnish with the basil. Serve at once.

cook's tip

There are many different types of clams found along almost every coast in the world. Those traditionally used in this dish are the tiny ones—only 1-2 inches across—known in Italy as vongole.

3

4

mussel & parsley conchiglie

Serve this aromatic seafood dish to family and friends who admit to a love of garlic.

Serves 4-6

2 lb 12 oz mussels

1 cup dry white wine

2 large onions, chopped

½ cup unsalted butter

6 large garlic cloves, finely chopped

5 tbsp chopped fresh parsley

1¼ cups heavy cream

14 oz dried pasta shells

1 tbsp olive oil

salt and pepper

crusty bread, to serve

1 Scrub and debeard the mussels under cold running water. Discard any that do not close immediately when sharply tapped. Put the mussels into a large pan, together with the wine and half of the onions. Cover and cook over a medium heat, shaking the pan frequently, for 2–3 minutes, or until the shells open.

2 Remove the pan from the heat. Drain the mussels and reserve the cooking liquid. Discard any mussels that have not opened. Strain the cooking liquid through a clean cloth into a glass pitcher or bowl and reserve.

1

3

3

cook's tip

Pasta shells are ideal because the sauce collects in the cavities and impregnates the pasta with flavor.

3 Melt the butter in a pan over a medium heat. Add the remaining onion and cook until translucent. Stir in the garlic and cook for 1 minute. Gradually stir in the reserved cooking liquid. Stir in the parsley and cream and season to taste with salt and black pepper. Simmer over a low heat.

4 Meanwhile, bring a large saucepan of lightly salted water to a boil. Add the pasta and olive oil and cook until just tender, but still firm to the bite. Drain the pasta and return to the pan. Cover and keep warm.

5 Reserve a few mussels for the garnish and remove the remainder from their shells. Stir the shelled mussels into the cream sauce and warm briefly.

6 Transfer the pasta to a large, warm serving dish. Pour over the sauce and toss well to coat. Garnish with the reserved mussels and serve with warm, crusty bread.

The pasta and rice recipes in this
chapter offer something special for every
occasion: filling vegetarian meals,
unusual vegetable side dishes, and main
courses. There are several innovative
new takes on the traditional Italian
favorite, the pizza, such as Calabrian,
and delicious salads making good use of local cheeses
such as Dolcelatte and Gorgonzola. Some of the dishes
included here are classics, while others are
imaginative and sometimes surprising new combinations

of vegetables and pasta. There are dishes
for every occasion from a cosy family
dinner to superb side dishes and splendid
vegetarian spreads.

vegetables
bakes & grains
pizzas

chile tagliatelle

A deliciously fresh and slightly spicy tomato sauce which is excellent for lunch or a light supper.

Serves 4

3 tbsp butter

1 onion, finely chopped

1 garlic clove, minced

2 small red chiles, seeded and diced

1 lb fresh tomatoes, skinned, seeded, and diced

¾ cup vegetable bouillon

2 tbsp tomato paste

1 tsp sugar

salt and pepper

1 lb 8 oz fresh green and white tagliatelle, or 12 oz dried

variation

Try topping your pasta dish with 1¾ oz pancetta or unsmoked bacon, diced and dry-fried for 5 minutes, o until crispy.

1 Melt the butter in a large pan. Add the onion and garlic and cook for 3–4 minutes, or until softened.

2 Add the chiles to the pan and continue cooking for about 2 minutes more.

3 Add the tomatoes and bouillon, then reduce the heat and let simmer for 10 minutes, stirring.

4 Pour the sauce into a food processor and blend for 1 minute, or until smooth. Alternatively, push the sauce through a strainer.

5 Return the sauce to the pan and add the tomato paste, sugar, and salt and pepper to taste. Gently reheat over a low heat, until piping hot.

6 Cook the tagliatelle in a pan of boiling water according to the instructions on the packet or until it is cooked, but still has bite. Drain the tagliatelle and transfer to serving plates. Serve with the tomato sauce.

1

2

3

tomato & anchovy penne

This Sicilian recipe of anchovies mixed with pine nuts and golden raisins in a tomato sauce is delicious with all types of pasta.

Serves 4

1lb tomatoes, halved

1 oz pine nuts

1¾ oz golden raisins

1¾ oz canned anchovies, drained and halved lengthwise

2 tbsp concentrated tomato paste

1lb 8 oz fresh or 12 oz dried penne

variation

Add 3½ oz bacon, broiled for 5 minutes until crispy, then chopped, instead of the anchovies, if you prefer.

1 Cook the tomatoes under a preheated broiler for about 10 minutes. Let cool. Once cool enough to handle, peel off the skin and dice the flesh.

2 Place the pine nuts on a cookie sheet and lightly toast under the broiler for 2–3 minutes, or until golden.

3 Soak the golden raisins in a bowl of warm water for about 20 minutes. Drain the golden raisins thoroughly.

4 Place the tomatoes, pine nuts, and golden raisins in a small pan and gently heat.

5 Add the anchovies and tomato paste, heating the sauce for an additional 2–3 minutes, or until hot.

6 Cook the pasta in a pan of lightly salted boiling water according to the instructions on the packet, or until it is cooked through, but still has bite. Drain thoroughly.

7 Transfer the pasta to a serving plate and serve with the hot sauce.

1

cook's tip

If you are making fresh pasta, remember that pasta dough prefers warm conditions and responds well to handling. Do not let chill and do not use a marble work surface for kneading.

3

5

tomato & arugula farfalle

The ingredients of this dish have the same bright colors as the Italian flag.

Serves 4

4 cups dried farfalle

4 tbsp olive oil

1 lb cherry tomatoes

3 oz arugula

salt and pepper

romano cheese, to garnish

1 Bring a large pan of lightly salted water to a boil. Add the farfalle and 1 tbsp of the olive oil and cook until tender, but still firm to the bite. Drain the farfalle thoroughly and return to the pan.

2 Cut the cherry tomatoes in half and trim the arugula.

3 Heat the remaining olive oil in a large pan. Add the tomatoes and cook for 1 minute. Add the farfalle and the arugula and stir gently to mix. Heat through and season to taste with salt and black pepper.

4 Meanwhile, using a vegetable peeler, shave thin slices of romano cheese.

5 Transfer the farfalle and vegetables to a warm serving dish. Garnish with the romano cheese shavings and serve immediately.

3

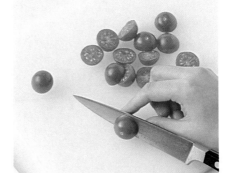

2

3

cook's tip

Arugula is a small plant with irregular-shaped leaves rather like those of greens. The flavor is distinctively peppery and slightly reminiscent of radish. It has always been popular in Italy, both in salads and for serving with pasta and has recently enjoyed a revival in Britain and the United States, where it has now become very fashionable.

cook's tip

Romano cheese is a hard sheep's milk cheese that resembles Parmesan and is often used for grating over a variety of dishes. It has a sharp flavor and is only used in small quantities.

pasta with classic pesto sauce

Delicious stirred into pasta, soups, and salad dressings, pesto is available in most supermarkets, but making your own gives a much fresher, fuller flavor.

Serves 4

about 40 fresh basil leaves, washed
   and dried
3 garlic cloves, minced
1 oz pine nuts
½ cup finely grated Parmesan cheese
2–3 tbsp extra virgin olive oil
salt and pepper
1 lb 8 oz fresh pasta or 12 oz dried pasta

1 Rinse the basil leaves and pat them dry with paper towels.

2 Put the basil leaves, garlic, pine nuts, and grated Parmesan into a food processor and blend for about 30 seconds, or until smooth. Alternatively, pound the ingredients by hand, using a mortar and pestle.

3 If you are using a food processor, keep the motor running and slowly add the olive oil. Alternatively, add the oil drop by drop while stirring briskly. Season with salt and pepper.

4 Meanwhile, cook the pasta in a saucepan of boiling water according to the instructions on the packet, or until it is cooked through, but still has bite. Drain.

5 Transfer the pasta to a serving plate and serve with the pesto. Toss to mix well and serve hot.

variation

Try making a walnut version of this pesto. Substitute 1 oz walnuts for the pine nuts and add 1 tablespoon walnut oil in step 2.

cook's tip

You can store pesto in the refrigerator for about 4 weeks. Cover the surface of the pesto with olive oil before sealing the container or bottle, to prevent the basil from oxidizing and turning black.

1

2

3

pasta crêpes with mushrooms & leeks

This vegetable crêpe can be filled with your favorite vegetables, as long as they are cooked beforehand. A favorite alternative is shredded parsnips dressed with 1 tablespoon of mustard.

Serves 4

2 corn cobs

4 tbsp butter

4 oz red bell peppers, cored, seeded and finely diced

2½ cups dried short-cut macaroni

⅔ cup heavy cream

¼ cup all-purpose flour

4 egg yolks

4 tbsp olive oil

salt and pepper

TO SERVE

oyster mushrooms

fried leeks

1 Bring a pan of water to a boil, then add the corn and cook for about 8 minutes. Drain thoroughly and refresh under cold running water for 3 minutes. Carefully cut away the kernels and set aside to dry.

2 Melt 2 tbsp of the butter in a skillet. Add the bell peppers and cook over a low heat for 4 minutes. Drain and pat dry with paper towels.

3 Bring a large pan of lightly salted water to a boil. Add the macaroni and cook for 12 minutes, or until tender but still firm to the bite. Drain the macaroni thoroughly and let cool in cold water until required.

4 Beat together the cream, flour, a pinch of salt, and the egg yolks in a bowl until smooth. Add the corn and bell peppers to the cream and egg mixture. Drain the macaroni and then toss into the corn and cream mixture. Season well with black pepper to taste.

5 Heat the remaining butter with the oil in a large skillet. Drop spoonfuls of the mixture into the pan and press down until the mixture forms a flat crêpe. Fry until golden on both sides and all the mixture is used up. Serve immediately with oyster mushrooms and fried leeks.

1

4

5

spinach & spring onion tagliatelle

A rich pasta dish for garlic lovers everywhere. It is quick and easy to prepare and full of flavor.

Serves 4

2 tbsp walnut oil

1 bunch scallions, sliced

2 garlic cloves, thinly sliced

3¼ cups sliced mushrooms

1 lb fresh green and white tagliatelle

1 tbsp olive oil

8 oz frozen spinach, thawed and drained

½ cup full-fat soft cheese with garlic and
    herbs

4 tbsp light cream

½ cup chopped, unsalted pistachio nuts

salt and pepper

TO GARNISH

2 tbsp shredded fresh basil

fresh basil sprigs

Italian bread, to serve

1 Heat the walnut oil in a large skillet. Add the scallions and garlic and cook for 1 minute, or until just softened.

2 Add the mushrooms to the pan and stir well. Cover and cook over a low heat for about 5 minutes, until softened.

3 Meanwhile, bring a large pan of lightly salted water to a boil. Add the tagliatelle and olive oil and cook for 3–5 minutes, or until tender but still firm to the bite. Drain the tagliatelle thoroughly and return to the pan.

4 Add the spinach to the skillet and heat through for 1–2 minutes. Add the cheese to the pan and let melt slightly. Stir in the cream and continue to cook, without letting the mixture come to a boil, until warmed through.

5 Pour the sauce over the pasta, then season to taste with salt and black pepper and mix well. Heat through gently, stirring constantly, for 2–3 minutes.

6 Transfer the pasta to a serving dish and sprinkle with the pistachio nuts and shredded basil. Garnish with the basil sprigs and serve immediately with the Italian bread of your choice.

2

4

5

eggplant bake with lamb sauce

Layers of toasty-brown eggplant, meat sauce, and cheese-flavored pasta make this a popular family supper dish.

Serves 4

1 eggplant, thinly sliced

5 tbsp olive oil

2 cups dried fusilli

2½ cups Béchamel sauce

¾ cup grated Cheddar cheese

butter, for greasing

⅛ cup freshly grated Parmesan cheese

salt and pepper

LAMB SAUCE

2 tbsp olive oil

1 large onion, sliced

2 celery stalks, thinly sliced

1 lb ground lamb

3 tbsp tomato paste

5½ oz bottled sun-dried tomatoes, drained and chopped

1 tsp dried oregano

1 tbsp red wine vinegar

⅝ cup chicken bouillon

salt and pepper

1 Put the eggplant slices in a colander, then sprinkle with salt and set aside for 45 minutes.

2 To make the lamb sauce, heat the oil in a pan. Fry the onion and celery for 3–4 minutes. Add the lamb and fry, stirring frequently, until browned. Stir in the remaining sauce ingredients, then bring to a boil and cook for 20 minutes.

3 Rinse the eggplant slices. Drain and pat dry. Heat 4 tbsp of the oil in a skillet. Fry the eggplant slices for about 4 minutes on each side. Remove from the pan and drain well.

3

5

4 Bring a large pan of lightly salted water to a boil. Add the fusilli and the remaining oil and cook until almost tender, but still firm to the bite. Drain well.

5 Gently heat the Béchamel sauce, stirring constantly. Stir in the Cheddar cheese. Stir half of the cheese sauce into the fusilli.

6 Make layers of fusilli, lamb sauce, and eggplant slices in a greased dish. Spread the remaining cheese sauce over the top. Sprinkle over the Parmesan and bake in a preheated oven at 375°F for 25 minutes. Serve hot or cold.

6

paglia e fieno

The name of this dish in Italian—paglia e fieno, "straw and hay"—refers to the colors of the pasta when mixed together.

Serves 4

4 tbsp butter

1 lb fresh peas, shelled

⅔ cup heavy cream

1 lb mixed fresh green and white spaghetti
   or tagliatelle

1 tbsp olive oil

⅔ cup freshly grated Parmesan cheese,
   plus extra to serve

pinch of freshly grated nutmeg

salt and pepper

1 Melt the butter in a large pan. Add the peas and cook, over a low heat, for 2–3 minutes.

2 Using a measuring cup, pour ⅝ cup of the cream into the pan. Bring to a boil and simmer for 1–1½ minutes, or until slightly thickened. Remove the pan from the heat.

3 Meanwhile, bring a large pan of lightly salted water to a boil. Add the spaghetti or tagliatelle and olive oil and cook for 2–3 minutes, or until just tender, but still firm to the bite. Remove the pan from the heat and drain the pasta thoroughly, then return to the pan.

1

2

4

4 Add the peas and cream sauce to the pasta. Return the pan to the heat, then add the remaining cream and the Parmesan cheese and season to taste with salt, black pepper, and freshly grated nutmeg.

5 Using 2 forks, gently toss the pasta to coat with the peas and cream sauce, while heating through.

6 Transfer the pasta to a serving dish and serve immediately, with extra Parmesan cheese.

variation

Fry 2 cups sliced button or oyster mushrooms in 4 tbsp butter over a low heat for 4-5 minutes. Stir into the peas and cream sauce just before adding to the pasta in step 4.

pumpkin & prosciutto tagliatelle

This unusual dish comes from the Emilia Romagna region. Why not serve it with Lambrusco, the local wine?

Serves 4

1 lb 2 oz pumpkin or butternut squash, peeled and seeded

3 tbsp olive oil

1 onion, finely chopped

2 garlic cloves, minced

4–6 tbsp chopped fresh parsley

pinch of freshly grated nutmeg

1¼ cups chicken or vegetable bouillon

4 oz prosciutto

9 oz dried tagliatelle

⅔ cup heavy cream

salt and pepper

freshly grated Parmesan cheese, to serve

1 Cut the pumpkin or butternut squash in half and scoop out the seeds with a spoon. Cut the pumpkin or squash into ½ inch dice.

2 Heat 2 tbsp of the olive oil in a large pan. Add the onion and garlic and fry over a low heat for about 3 minutes, or until soft. Add half the parsley and cook for 1 minute.

3 Add the pumpkin or squash pieces and cook for 2–3 minutes. Season to taste with salt, pepper, and nutmeg.

4 Add half the bouillon to the pan and bring to a boil, then cover and simmer for about 10 minutes, or until the pumpkin or squash is tender. Add more bouillon if the pumpkin or squash is becoming dry and looks as if it might burn.

5 Add the prosciutto to the pan and cook, stirring frequently, for an additional 2 minutes.

6 Meanwhile, bring a large pan of lightly salted water to a boil. Add the tagliatelle and the remaining oil and cook for 12 minutes, or until tender, but still firm to the bite. Drain the pasta and transfer to a warm serving dish.

7 Stir the cream into the pumpkin and ham mixture and heat through. Spoon over the pasta, then sprinkle over the remaining parsley and serve. Hand the grated Parmesan separately.

1   5   7

creamy walnut & olive pasta

This mouthwatering dish would make an excellent light, vegetarian lunch for four or a good appetizer for six.

Serves 4-6

2 thick slices whole-wheat bread,
    crusts removed

1¼ cups milk

2½ cups shelled walnuts

2 garlic cloves, minced

1 cup pitted black olives

¼ cup freshly grated Parmesan cheese

8 tbsp extra virgin olive oil

¼ cup heavy cream

1 lb fresh fettuccine

salt and pepper

2–3 tbsp chopped fresh parsley

1 Put the bread in a shallow dish. Pour over the milk and set aside to soak until the liquid has been absorbed.

2 Spread the walnuts out on a cookie sheet and toast in a preheated oven at 375°F for about 5 minutes, or until golden. Set aside to cool.

3 Put the soaked bread, walnuts, garlic, olives, Parmesan cheese, and 6 tbsp of the olive oil in a food processor and work to make a paste. Season to taste with salt and black pepper and stir in the cream.

4 Bring a large pan of lightly salted water to a boil. Add the fettuccine and 1 tbsp of the remaining oil and cook for 2–3 minutes, or until tender but still firm to the bite. Drain the fettuccine thoroughly and toss with the remaining olive oil.

5 Divide the fettuccine between individual serving plates and spoon the olive, garlic, and walnut sauce on top. Sprinkle over the fresh parsley and serve immediately.

3

cook's tip

Parmesan quickly loses its pungency and bite. It is better to buy small quantities and grate it yourself. Wrapped in foil, it will keep in the refrigerator for several months.

1

3

casseroled beans & penne with herbs

A satisfying winter dish, this pasta and bean casserole with a crunchy topping is a slow-cooked, one-pot meal.

Serves 6

1¼ cups dried navy beans, soaked overnight and drained

8 oz dried penne

6 tbsp olive oil

3½ cups vegetable bouillon

2 large onions, sliced

2 garlic cloves, chopped

2 bay leaves

1 tsp dried oregano

1 tsp dried thyme

5 tbsp red wine

2 tbsp tomato paste

2 celery stalks, sliced

1 fennel bulb, sliced

1¾ cups sliced mushrooms

8 oz tomatoes, sliced

1 tsp dark muscovado sugar

4 tbsp dry white bread crumbs

salt and pepper

salad greens and crusty bread, to serve

1 Put the navy beans in a large pan and add sufficient cold water to cover. Bring to a boil and continue to boil vigorously for 20 minutes. Drain, set aside, and keep warm.

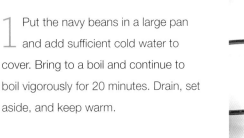

2 Bring a large pan of lightly salted water to a boil. Add the penne and 1 tbsp of the olive oil and cook for about 3 minutes. Drain the pasta. Set aside and keep warm.

3 Put the beans in a large, flameproof casserole. Add the vegetable bouillon and stir in the remaining olive oil,

3

3

the onions, garlic, bay leaves, oregano, thyme, wine, and tomato paste. Bring to a boil, then cover and cook in a heated oven at 350°F for 2 hours.

4 Add the penne, celery, fennel, mushrooms, and tomatoes to the casserole and season to taste with salt and pepper. Stir in the muscovado sugar and sprinkle over the bread crumbs. Cover the dish and cook in the oven for 1 more hour.

5 Serve hot with salad greens and crusty bread.

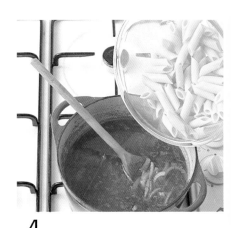

4

fennel & bacon pasta

This aniseed-flavored vegetable gives that extra punch to this delicious creamy pasta dish.

Serves 4

6 fennel bulbs

¼ cup vegetable bouillon

2 tbsp butter

6 strips rindless smoked bacon, diced

6 shallots, cut into fourths

¼ cup all-purpose flour

7 tbsp heavy cream

1 tbsp Madeira wine

1 lb dried linguine

1 tbsp olive oil

salt and pepper

1 Trim the fennel bulbs, then gently peel off and reserve the first layer of the bulbs. Cut the bulbs into fourths and put them in a large pan, together with the vegetable bouillon and the reserved outer layers. Bring to a boil, then lower the heat and simmer for 5 minutes.

2 Using a draining spoon, transfer the fennel to a large dish. Discard the outer layers of the fennel bulb. Bring the vegetable bouillon to a boil and let it reduce by half. Set aside.

3 Melt the butter in a skillet. Add the bacon and shallots and cook for 4 minutes. Add the flour, reduced bouillon, cream, and Madeira and cook, stirring constantly, for 3 minutes, or until the sauce is smooth. Season with salt and black pepper and pour over the fennel.

4 Bring a large pan of lightly salted water to a boil. Add the linguine and olive oil and cook for 10 minutes, or until tender, but still firm to the bite. Drain and transfer to a deep ovenproof dish.

5 Add the fennel and sauce and braise in a preheated oven at 350°F for 20 minutes. Serve immediately.

cook's tip

Fennel will keep in the salad drawer of the refrigerator for 2-3 days, but it is best eaten as fresh as possible. Cut surfaces turn brown quickly, so do not prepare it too much in advance of cooking.

3

1

3

vegetable lasagna with two cheeses

This rich, baked pasta dish is packed full of vegetables, tomatoes, and Italian mozzarella cheese.

Serves 6

2 lb 4 oz eggplant

8 tbsp olive oil

2 tbsp garlic and herb butter

1 lb zucchini, sliced

2 cups grated mozzarella cheese

2½ cups strained tomatoes

6 sheets pre-cooked green lasagna

2½ cups Béchamel Sauce

¾ cup freshly grated Parmesan cheese

1 tsp dried oregano

salt and black pepper

1

1 Thinly slice the eggplant and place in a colander. Sprinkle with salt and set aside for 20 minutes. Rinse and pat dry with paper towels.

2 Heat 4 tbsp of the oil in a large skillet. Cook half the eggplant slices over a low heat for 6–7 minutes, or until golden. Drain well on paper towels. Repeat with the remaining oil and eggplant slices.

3 Melt the garlic and herb butter in the skillet. Add the zucchini and cook for 5–6 minutes, or until golden brown all over. Drain on paper towels.

4

5

4 Place half the eggplant and zucchini slices in a large ovenproof dish. Season with pepper and sprinkle over half the mozzarella cheese. Spoon over half the strained tomatoes and top with 3 sheets of lasagna. Repeat the process, ending with a layer of lasagna.

5 Spoon over the Béchamel sauce and sprinkle over the Parmesan cheese and oregano. Put the dish on a cookie sheet and bake in a preheated oven at 425°F for 30–35 minutes, or until golden brown. Serve immediately.

mixed vegetable ravioli

It is important not to overcook the vegetable filling or it will become sloppy and unexciting, instead of firm to the bite and delicious.

1

Serves 4

1 lb Basic Pasta Dough (see page 7)

1 tbsp olive oil

6 tbsp butter

¼ cup light cream

1 cup freshly grated Parmesan cheese

STUFFING

2 large eggplant

3 large zucchini

6 large tomatoes

1 large green bell pepper

1 large red bell pepper

3 garlic cloves

1 large onion

½ cup olive oil

2 oz tomato paste

½ tsp chopped fresh basil

salt and pepper

2

1 To make the stuffing, cut the eggplant and zucchini into 1 inch chunks. Put the eggplant pieces in a colander, then sprinkle with salt and set aside for 20 minutes. Rinse and drain.

2 Blanch the tomatoes in boiling water for 2 minutes. Drain, skin, and chop the flesh. Core and seed the bell peppers and cut into 1 inch dice. Chop the garlic and onion.

3 Heat the oil in a saucepan. Add the garlic and onion and cook for 3 minutes. Stir in the eggplant, zucchini, tomatoes, bell peppers, tomato paste, and basil. Season with salt and pepper, then cover and simmer for 20 minutes, stirring frequently.

3

4 Roll out the pasta dough and cut out 3 inch circles with a plain cutter. Put a spoonful of the vegetable stuffing on each round. Dampen the edges slightly and fold the pasta rounds over, pressing together to seal.

5 Bring a saucepan of salted water to a boil. Add the ravioli and the oil and cook for 3–4 minutes. Drain and transfer to a greased ovenproof dish, dotting each layer with butter. Pour over the cream and sprinkle over the Parmesan cheese. Bake in a preheated oven at 400°F for 20 minutes. Serve hot.

stir-fried vegetables with conchiglie

Prepare all the vegetables and cook the pasta in advance, then the dish can be cooked in a few minutes.

Serves 4

14 oz dried whole-wheat pasta shells or
   other short pasta shapes

1 tbsp olive oil

2 carrots, thinly sliced

4 oz baby corn cobs

3 tbsp corn oil

1 inch piece fresh gingerroot, thinly sliced

1 large onion, thinly sliced

1 garlic clove, thinly sliced

3 celery stalks, thinly sliced

1 small red bell pepper, cored, seeded,
   and cut into short, thin sticks

1 small green bell pepper, cored, seeded,
   and cut into short, thin sticks

1 tsp cornstarch

2 tbsp water

3 tbsp soy sauce

3 tbsp dry sherry

1 tsp honey

a dash of hot pepper sauce (optional)

salt

1 Bring a large pan of lightly salted water to a boil. Add the pasta and olive oil and cook until tender, but still firm to the bite. Drain, then return to the pan and keep warm.

2 Bring a pan of lightly salted water to a boil. Add the carrots and corn and cook for 2 minutes. Drain, then refresh in cold water and drain again.

3 Heat the corn oil in a preheated wok or large skillet. Add the ginger and stir-fry over a medium heat for 1 minute to flavor the oil. Remove the ginger with a draining spoon and discard.

4 Add the onion, garlic, celery, and bell peppers to the pan and stir-fry for 2 minutes. Add the carrots and baby corn and stir-fry for 2 minutes. Stir in the cooked pasta.

5 Mix together the cornstarch and water to make a smooth paste. Stir in the soy sauce, sherry, and honey. Pour the cornstarch mixture into the pasta and cook, stirring occasionally, for 2 minutes. Stir in a dash of pepper sauce, if liked. Transfer to a serving dish and serve immediately.

4

4

5

baby eggplant & artichoke pasta

Delicious Mediterranean vegetables, cooked in rich tomato sauce, make an ideal topping for nutty whole-wheat pasta.

Serves 4

2 tbsp olive oil

1 large, red onion, chopped

2 garlic cloves, minced

1 tbsp lemon juice

4 baby eggplant, cut into fourths

2¼ cups strained tomatoes

2 tsp superfine sugar

2 tbsp tomato paste

14 oz canned artichoke hearts, drained and halved

1 cup pitted black olives

12 oz dried spaghetti

2 tbsp butter

salt and pepper

fresh basil sprigs, to garnish

olive bread, to serve

1 Heat 1 tbsp of the olive oil in a large skillet. Add the onion, garlic, lemon juice, and eggplant and cook over a low heat for 4–5 minutes, or until the onion and eggplant are lightly golden brown.

2 Pour in the strained tomatoes, season to taste with salt and black pepper and stir in the superfine sugar and tomato paste. Bring to a boil, then lower the heat and simmer, stirring occasionally, for 20 minutes.

3 Gently stir in the artichoke hearts and black olives and cook for 5 minutes.

4 Meanwhile, bring a large saucepan of lightly salted water to a boil. Add the spaghetti and the remaining oil and cook for 7–8 minutes, or until tender, but still firm to the bite.

5 Drain the spaghetti and toss with the butter. Transfer the spaghetti to a large serving dish.

6 Pour the vegetable sauce over the spaghetti and garnish with the sprigs of fresh basil. Serve immediately with olive bread.

2

3

5

baked mushroom & pasta flan

Lightly cooked vermicelli is pressed into a flan ring and baked with a creamy mushroom filling.

Serves 4

6 tbsp butter, plus extra, for greasing

8 oz dried vermicelli or spaghetti

1 tbsp olive oil

1 onion, chopped

5 oz button mushrooms

1 green bell pepper, cored, seeded,
    and sliced into thin rings

¼ cup milk

3 eggs, lightly beaten

2 tbsp heavy cream

1 tsp dried oregano

freshly grated nutmeg

1 tbsp freshly grated Parmesan cheese

salt and pepper

tomato and basil salad, to serve

1 Generously grease an 8 inch loose-based flan pan with butter.

2 Bring a large pan of lightly salted water to a boil. Add the vermicelli and olive oil and cook until tender, but still firm to the bite. Drain, then return to the pan. Add 2 tbsp of the butter and shake the pan to coat the pasta.

3

5

5

3 Press the pasta on to the base and around the sides of the flan pan to make a flan case.

4 Melt the remaining butter in a skillet over a medium heat. Add the onion and cook until it is translucent.

5 Add the mushrooms and bell pepper rings to the skillet and cook, stirring, for 2–3 minutes. Spoon the onion, mushroom, and bell pepper mixture into the flan case and press it into the base.

6 Beat together the milk, eggs, and cream, then stir in the oregano and season to taste with nutmeg and black pepper. Carefully pour the mixture over the vegetables and sprinkle over the cheese.

7 Bake the flan in a preheated oven at 350°F for 40–45 minutes, or until the filling has set.

8 Slide the flan out of the pan and serve warm, accompanied by a tomato and basil salad.

chicken, leek & peanut risotto

If you prefer, ordinary long grain rice can be used instead of risotto rice, but it won't give you the traditional, deliciously creamy texture that is typical of Italian risottos.

Serves 4

2 tbsp sunflower oil

1 tbsp butter or margarine

1 medium leek, thinly sliced

1 large yellow bell pepper, diced

3 skinless, boneless chicken breasts, diced

12 oz round grain rice

few strands saffron

6¼ cups chicken bouillon

7 oz canned corn cob

½ cup toasted unsalted peanuts

½ cup grated Parmesan cheese

salt and pepper

1 Heat the oil and butter or margarine in a large pan. Cook the leek and bell pepper for 1 minute, then stir in the chicken and cook, stirring until golden brown.

1

2 Stir in the rice and cook for about 2–3 minutes.

3 Stir in the saffron strands, and salt and pepper to taste. Add the bouillon, a little at a time, then cover and cook over a low heat, stirring ccasionally, for about 20 minutes, or until the rice is tender and most of the liquid is absorbed. Do not let the risotto dry out— add more bouillon if necessary.

4 Stir in the corn cob, peanuts, and Parmesan cheese, then adjust the seasoning to taste. Serve hot.

cook's tip

Risottos can be frozen, before adding the Parmesan cheese, for up to 1 month, but remember to reheat this risotto thoroughly as it contains chicken.

2

4

basil & tomato bread

This delicious tomato bread is great with cheese or soup or to make an unusual sandwich.

makes 1 loaf

¼ oz dried yeast

1 tsp sugar

1¼ cups hand-hot water

1 lb strong white flour

1 tsp salt

2 tsp dried basil

2 tbsp sun-dried tomato paste or
    tomato paste

12 sun-dried tomatoes, cut into strips

cook's tip

You could make mini sun-dried tomato loaves for children. Divide the dough into 8 equal portions, let rise and bake in mini-loaf pans for 20 minutes. Alternatively, make 12 small rounds, leave to rise and bake as rolls for 12-15 minutes.

1 Place the yeast and sugar in a bowl and mix with 8 tablespoons of the water. Let ferment in a warm place for 15 minutes.

2 Place the flour in a bowl and stir in the salt. Make a well in the dry ingredients and add the basil, the yeast mixture, tomato paste, and half of the remaining water. Using a wooden spoon, draw the flour into the liquid and mix to form a dough, adding the rest of the water gradually.

3 Turn out the dough on to a floured surface and knead for 5 minutes, or until smooth. Cover with oiled plastic wrap and let stand in a warm place to rise for about 30 minutes, or until doubled in size.

4 Lightly grease a 2 lb loaf pan.

6

5 Remove the dough from the bowl and knead in the sun-dried tomatoes. Knead again for 2–3 minutes.

6 Place the dough in the pan and let rise for 30–40 minutes. Once it has doubled in size again, bake in a preheated oven at 375°F for 30–35 minutes, or until golden and the base sounds hollow when tapped.

2

5

focaccia with romano cheese

This flat cheese bread is sometimes called foccacia. It is delicious served with antipasto or simply on its own.

Makes 1 loaf

/ oz dried yeast

1 tsp sugar

1 cup hand-hot water

12 oz strong flour

1 tsp salt

3 tbsp olive oil

7 oz romano cheese, cubed

/ tbsp fennel seeds, lightly minced

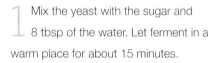

3

1 Mix the yeast with the sugar and 8 tbsp of the water. Let ferment in a warm place for about 15 minutes.

2 Mix the flour with the salt. Add 1 tbsp of the oil, the yeast mixture, and the remaining water to form a smooth dough. Knead the dough for 4 minutes.

3 Divide the dough into 2 equal portions. Roll out each portion to a form a circle ¼ inch thick. Place 1 circle on a cookie sheet. Scatter the cheese and half of the fennel seeds evenly over the round.

4 Place the second circle on top and squeeze the edges together to seal so that the filling does not leak out during cooking.

5 Using a sharp knife, make a few slashes in the top of the dough and brush with the remaining olive oil.

6 Sprinkle with the remaining fennel seeds and let rise for 20–30 minutes.

7 Bake in a preheated oven at 400°F for 30 minutes, or until golden. Serve immediately.

cook's tip

Romano is a hard, quite salty cheese, which is sold in most large supermarkets and Italian delicatessens. If you cannot obtain it, use strong Cheddar or Parmesan cheese instead.

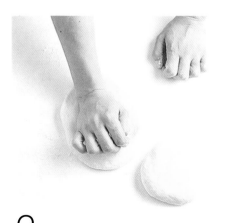

2

4

roasted bell pepper & rosemary bread

Bell peppers become sweet and mild when they are roasted and make this bread delicious.

Serves 4

1 red bell pepper, halved and seeded

1 yellow bell pepper, halved and seeded

2 sprigs rosemary

1 tbsp olive oil

¼ oz dried yeast

1 tsp sugar

1¼ cups hand-hot water

1 lb strong white flour

1 tsp salt

1 Grease a 9 inch deep round cake pan.

2 Place the bell peppers and rosemary in a shallow roasting pan. Pour over the oil and roast in a preheated oven, at 400°F, for 20 minutes, or until slightly charred. Remove the skin from the bell peppers and cut the flesh into slices.

3 Place the yeast and sugar in a small bowl and mix with 8 tablespoons of hand-hot water. Let ferment in a warm place for about 15 minutes.

4 Mix the flour and salt together in a large bowl. Stir in the yeast mixture and the remaining water and mix to form a smooth dough.

5 Knead the dough for 5 minutes, or until smooth. Cover with oiled plastic wrap and let rise for about 30 minutes, or until doubled in size.

6 Cut the dough into 3 equal portions. Roll the portions into circles slightly larger than the cake pan.

7 Place 1 circle in the base of the pan so that it reaches up the sides of the pan by about ¾ inch. Top with half of the bell pepper mixture.

8 Place the second circle of dough on top, followed by the remaining bell pepper mixture. Place the last round of dough on top, pushing the edges of the dough down the sides of the pan.

9 Cover the dough with oiled plastic wrap and let rise for 30–40 minutes. Place in the preheated oven and bake for 45 minutes until golden or the base sounds hollow when lightly tapped. Serve warm.

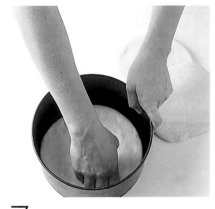

7

2

6

onion focaccia with rosemary

Onion focaccia makes a delicious snack on its own, or serve it with cured meats and salad for a quick supper.

Makes 16 squares

1/4 oz dried yeast

1 tsp sugar

1¼ cups hand-hot water

1 lb strong white flour

2 tsp salt

3 tbsp rosemary, chopped

2 tbsp olive oil

1 lb mixed red and white onions, sliced
   into rings

4 garlic cloves, sliced

1 Place the yeast and the sugar in a small bowl and mix with 8 tablespoons of the water. Let ferment in a warm place for 15 minutes.

2 Mix the flour with the salt in a large bowl. Add the yeast mixture, half of the rosemary, and the remaining water and mix to form a smooth dough. Knead the dough for 4 minutes.

3 Cover the dough with oiled plastic wrap and let rise for 30 minutes, or until doubled in size.

4 Meanwhile, heat the oil in a large pan. Add the onions and garlic and cook for 5 minutes, or until softened. Cover the pan and continue to cook for an additional 7–8 minutes, or until the onions are lightly caramelized.

5 Remove the dough from the bowl and knead it again for 1–2 minutes.

6 Roll the dough out to form a square shape. The dough should be no more than ¼ inch thick because it will rise during cooking. Place the dough onto a large cookie sheet, pushing out the edges until even.

7 Spread the onions over the dough and sprinkle with the remaining chopped rosemary.

8 Bake in a preheated oven 400°F for 25–30 minutes, or until golden. Cut into 16 squares and serve immediately.

2

4

6

italian pissaladière

This pizza, similar to the French Pissaladière, is made with a pastry base flavored with cheese and topped with a delicious tomato sauce and roasted bell peppers.

Serves 4

1½ cups all-purpose flour

4½ oz butter, diced

½ tsp salt

2 tbsp dried Parmesan cheese

1 egg, beaten

2 tbsp cold water

2 tbsp olive oil

1 large onion, finely chopped

1 garlic clove, chopped

14 oz canned chopped tomatoes

4 tbsp concentrated tomato paste

1 red bell pepper, halved

5 sprigs of thyme, stalks removed

6 black olives, pitted and halved

1/4 cup grated Parmesan cheese

1 Sift the flour and rub in the butter to make bread crumbs. Stir in the salt and dried Parmesan. Add the egg and 1 tablespoon of the water and mix with a round-bladed knife. Add more water if necessary to make a soft dough. Cover with plastic wrap and chill for at least 30 minutes.

2 Meanwhile, heat the oil in a skillet and cook the onions and garlic for about 5 minutes, or until golden. Add the tomatoes and cook for 8–10 minutes. Stir in the tomato paste.

3 Place the bell peppers, skin-side up, on a cookie sheet and cook under a preheated broiler for 15 minutes, or until charred. Place in a plastic bag and let sweat for 10 minutes. Peel off the skin and slice the flesh into thin strips.

4 Roll out the dough to fit a 9 inch loose base fluted flan pan. Line with foil and bake in a preheated oven at 400°F for 10 minutes, or until just set. Remove the foil and bake for an additional 5 minutes, or until lightly golden. Let cool slightly.

5 Spoon the tomato sauce over the pastry base and top with the bell peppers, thyme, olives, and fresh Parmesan. Return to the oven for 15 minutes, or until the pastry is crisp. Serve warm or cold.

1

1

3

cheese & tomato pizza

Pizza means "pie" in Italian. The fresh bread dough is not difficult to make, but it does take a little time.

Serves 4

BASIC PIZZA DOUGH

¼ oz dried yeast

1 tsp sugar

1 cup hand-hot water

12 oz strong flour

1 tsp salt

1 tbsp olive oil

TOPPING

14 oz canned tomatoes, chopped

2 garlic cloves, minced

2 tsp dried basil

1 tbsp olive oil

2 tbsp tomato paste

3½ oz mozzarella cheese, chopped

2 tbsp freshly grated Parmesan cheese

salt and pepper

2

3

1

1 Place the yeast and sugar in a pitcher and mix with 4 tbsp of the water. Let the yeast mixture stand in a warm place for 15 minutes, or until frothy.

2 Mix the flour with the salt and make a well in the center. Add the oil, the yeast mixture, and the remaining water. Using a wooden spoon, mix together to form a dough.

3 Turn the dough out on to a floured counter and knead for 4–5 minutes, or until smooth.

4 Return the dough to the bowl, then cover with an oiled sheet of plastic wrap and let rise for 30 minutes, or until doubled in size.

5 Knead the dough for 2 minutes. Stretch the dough with your hands, then place it on an oiled cookie sheet, pushing out the edges until even and to the shape required. The dough should be no more than ¼ inch thick because it will rise during cooking.

6 To make the topping, place the tomatoes, garlic, dried basil, olive oil, and salt and pepper to taste in a large skillet and let simmer for 20 minutes, or until the sauce has thickened. Stir in the tomato paste and let cool slightly.

7 Spread the topping evenly over the pizza base. Top with the mozzarella and Parmesan cheeses and bake in a preheated oven at 400°F for 20–25 minutes. Serve hot.

calabrian pizza

This is a traditional dish from the Calabrian Mountains in southern Italy, where it is made with naturally sun-dried tomatoes and ricotta cheese.

Serves 4

1 portion Basic Pizza Dough (see page 328)

TOPPING

4 tbsp sun-dried tomato paste

5½ oz ricotta cheese

10 sun-dried tomatoes

1 tbsp fresh thyme

salt and pepper

1 Knead the dough for 2 minutes.

2 Using a rolling pin, roll out the dough to form a circle, then place it on an oiled cookie sheet, pushing out the edges until even. The dough should be no more than ¼ inch thick because it will rise during cooking.

3 Spread the sun-dried tomato paste over the dough, then add spoonfuls of ricotta.

4 Cut the sun-dried tomatoes into strips and arrange these on top of the pizza.

5 Sprinkle the thyme, and salt and pepper to taste over the top of the pizza. Bake in a preheated oven at 400°F for 30 minutes or until the crust is golden. Serve hot.

3

cook's tip

The dough for crispy-based pizzas should be rolled out as thinly as possible.

2

roman pizza

This pizza is a favorite of the Romans. It is slightly unusual because the topping is made without a tomato sauce base.

2

2

4

Serves 4

1 portion of Basic Pizza Dough

(see page 328)

TOPPING

2 tbsp olive oil

9 oz onions, sliced into rings

2 garlic cloves, minced

1 red bell pepper, diced

3½ oz prosciutto, cut into strips

3½ oz mozzarella cheese, sliced

2 tbsp rosemary, stalks removed and

roughly chopped

1 Remove the dough from the bowl. Knead the dough for 2 minutes. Using a rolling pin, roll out the dough to form a square shape, then place it on an oiled cookie sheet, pushing out the edges until even. The dough should be no more than ¼ inch thick because it will rise during cooking.

2 To make the topping, heat the oil in a pan. Add the onions and garlic and cook for 3 minutes. Add the bell pepper and fry for a further 2 minutes.

3 Cover the pan and cook the vegetables over a low heat for 10 minutes, stirring occasionally, until the onions are slightly caramelized. Leave to cool slightly.

4 Spread the topping evenly over the pizza base. Place strips of prosciutto, mozzarella, and rosemary over the top. Bake in a preheated oven at 400°F for 20–25 minutes. Serve hot.

mushroom & mozzarella pizza

Juicy mushrooms and stringy mozzarella top this tomato-based pizza. Use exotic mushrooms or a combination of exotic and cultivated mushrooms.

Serves 4

1 portion Basic Pizza Dough (see page 328)

TOPPING

14 oz canned chopped tomatoes

2 garlic cloves, minced

1 tsp dried basil

1 tbsp olive oil

2 tbsp tomato paste

7 oz mushrooms

5½ oz mozzarella cheese, grated

salt and pepper

basil leaves, to garnish

1 Knead the dough for 2 minutes. Using a rolling pin, roll out the dough to form an oval or a circular shape, then place it on an oiled cookie sheet, pushing out the edges until even. The dough should be no more than ¼ inch thick because it rises while cooking.

2 Using a sharp knife, chop the mushrooms into slices.

3 To make the topping, place the tomatoes, garlic, dried basil, olive oil, and salt and pepper in a large pan and simmer for 20 minutes, or until the sauce has thickened. Stir in the tomato paste and let cool slightly.

4 Spread the sauce over the base of the pizza, then top with the sliced mushrooms and scatter over the mozzarella.

5 Bake in a preheated oven at 400°F for 25 minutes. Just before serving, garnish with fresh basil leaves.

3

3

2

pancetta & olive pizette

Pizette, as they are known in Italy, are tiny pizzas. This quantity will make 8 individual pizzas, or 16 cocktail pizzas to go with drinks.

Serves 4

1 portion Basic Pizza Dough (see page 328)

TOPPING

2 zucchini

3½ oz tomato paste

2¼ oz pancetta, diced

1¼ oz black olives, pitted and chopped

1 tbsp mixed dried herbs

2 tbsp olive oil

1

2

3

1 Knead the dough for 2 minutes and divide it into 8 balls. Roll out each portion thinly to form circles or squares, then place them on an oiled cookie sheet, pushing out the edges until even. The dough should be no more than ¼ inch thick because it will rise during cooking.

2 To make the topping, grate the zucchini finely. Cover with paper towels and let stand for 10 minutes to absorb some of the juices.

3 Spread 2–3 teaspoons of the tomato paste over the pizza bases and top each with the grated zucchini, pancetta, and olives. Season with freshly ground black pepper and a sprinkling of mixed dried herbs, then drizzle with olive oil.

4 Bake in a preheated oven at 400°F for 15 minutes, or until crispy. Season and serve hot.

pizza tartlets

This is a traditional pizza which uses a pastry case and béchamel sauce to make a type of savory flan. Grating the pastry gives it a lovely nutty texture.

Serves 4

9 oz flaky pastry, well chilled

3 tbsp butter

1 red onion, chopped

1 garlic clove, chopped

1½ oz strong flour

1¼ cups milk

½ cup finely grated Parmesan cheese,
    plus extra for sprinkling

2 eggs, hard-cooked, cut into fourths

3½ oz Italian pork sausage, such as salami,
    cut into strips

salt and pepper

sprigs of fresh thyme, to garnish

1 Fold the sheet of flaky pastry in half and coarsely grate it into 4 individual flan pans, 4 inches across. Using a floured fork, press the pastry flakes down lightly so that they are even, there are no holes, and the pastry comes up the sides of the pan.

2 Line with foil and bake blind in a preheated oven at 425°F for 10 minutes. Reduce the heat to 400°F, and remove the foil, then cook for an additional 15 minutes, or until golden and set.

3 Heat the butter in a pan. Add the onion and garlic and cook for 5–6 minutes or until softened.

4 Add the flour, stirring well to coat the onions. Gradually stir in the milk to make a thick sauce. Season well with salt and pepper and then stir in the Parmesan cheese. Do not reheat once the cheese has been added or the sauce will become stringy.

5 Spread the sauce over the pastry cases. Decorate with the egg and strips of sausage.

6 Sprinkle with a little extra Parmesan cheese, return to the oven and bake for 5 minutes, just to heat through.

7 Serve immediately, garnished with sprigs of fresh thyme.

cook's tip

This pizza is just as good cold, but do not prepare it too far in advance, as the pastry will become soggy.

1

1

4

mortadella calzone

A calzone, as this pizza is known, can have many different fillings. Here, cured meats mix well with mozzarella and Parmesan cheese.

Makes 4 large or 8 small calzone

1 portion of Basic Pizza Dough
   (see page 328)
freshly grated Parmesan cheese, to serve

TOPPING

2¾ oz mortadella or other Italian pork
   sausage, chopped
1¼ oz Italian sausage, chopped
1¼ oz Parmesan cheese, sliced
3½ oz mozzarella, cut into chunks
2 tomatoes, diced
4 tbsp fresh oregano
salt and pepper

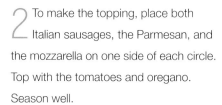

2

3

1 Knead the dough for 2 minutes and divide it into 4 pieces. Roll out each portion thinly to form circles. Place them on an oiled cookie sheet. The dough should be no more than ¼ inch thick because it will rise during cooking.

2 To make the topping, place both Italian sausages, the Parmesan, and the mozzarella on one side of each circle. Top with the tomatoes and oregano. Season well.

3 Brush around the edges of the dough with a little water, then fold over the circle to form a pasty shape. Squeeze the edges together to seal so that none of the filling leaks out during cooking.

4 Bake in a preheated oven at 400°F for 10–15 minutes, or until golden. If you are making the smaller pizzas, reduce the cooking time to 8–10 minutes. Serve with freshly grated Parmesan cheese.

1

grilled peaches with maple syrup

If you prepare these in advance, all you have to do is pop the peaches on the grill when you are ready to serve them.

1

2

3

Serves 4

4 peaches

6 oz mascarpone cheese

1½ oz pecan or walnuts, chopped

1 tsp sunflower oil

4 tbsp maple syrup

1 Cut the peaches in half and remove the pits. If you are preparing this recipe in advance, press the peach halves together again and wrap them in plastic wrap until required.

2 Mix the mascarpone and pecan or walnuts together in a small bowl until well combined. Let chill in the refrigerator until required.

3 To serve, brush the peaches with a little oil and place on a rack set over medium-hot coals. Grill the peach halves for 5–10 minutes, turning once, until hot.

4 Transfer the peach halves to a serving dish and top with the mascarpone and nut mixture.

5 Drizzle the maple syrup over the peaches and mascarpone filling and serve at once.

variation

You can use nectarines instead of peaches for this recipe, if you prefer. Remember to choose ripe but fairly firm fruit which won't go soft and mushy when it is grilled. Prepare the nectarines in the same way as the peaches and grill for 5–10 minutes.

cook's tip

Mascarpone cheese is high in fat, so if you are following a low-fat diet, use thick natural yogurt instead.

raspberry almond spirals

This is the ultimate in self-indulgence—a truly delicious dessert that tastes every bit as good as it looks.

Serves 4

½ cup fusilli

4 cups raspberries

2 tbsp superfine sugar

1 tbsp lemon juice

4 tbsp slivered almonds

3 tbsp raspberry liqueur

1 Bring a large pan of lightly salted water to a boil. Add the fusilli and cook until tender, but still firm to the bite. Drain the fusilli thoroughly, then return to the pan and set aside to cool.

2 Using a spoon, firmly press 1⅓ cups of the raspberries through a strainer set over a large mixing bowl to form a smooth paste.

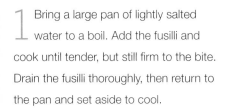

3 Put the raspberry paste and sugar in a small pan and simmer over a low heat, stirring occasionally, for 5 minutes. Stir in the lemon juice and set the sauce aside until required.

4 Add the remaining raspberries to the fusilli in the pan and mix together well. Transfer the raspberry and fusilli mixture to a serving dish.

5 Spread the almonds out on a cookie sheet and toast under the broiler until golden brown. Remove and set aside to cool slightly.

6 Stir the raspberry liqueur into the reserved raspberry sauce and mix together well until very smooth. Pour the raspberry sauce over the fusilli, then generously sprinkle over the toasted almonds and serve.

cook's tip

You could use almost any sweet, really ripe berry for making this dessert. Strawberries and blackberries are especially suitable, combined with the correspondingly flavored liqueur. Alternatively, you could use a different berry mixed with the fusilli, but still pour over the raspberry sauce.

sweet chestnut & almond parcels

These scrumptious little parcels are the perfect dessert for anyone with a really sweet tooth.

Serves 4

PASTA

3¾ cups all-purpose flour

10 tbsp butter, plus extra for greasing

¼ cup superfine sugar

4 eggs

1 oz yeast

½ cup warm milk

FILLING

½ cup chestnut paste

½ cup cocoa powder

¼ cup superfine sugar

½ cup chopped almonds

1 cup crushed amaretti cookies

⅓ cup orange marmalade

3

4

8

1 To make the sweet pasta dough, sift the flour into a mixing bowl, then mix in the butter, sugar, and 3 eggs.

2 Mix together the yeast and warm milk in a small bowl and when thoroughly combined, mix into the dough.

3 Knead the dough for 20 minutes. Cover with a clean cloth and set aside in a warm place for 1 hour to rise.

4 Mix together the chestnut paste, cocoa powder, sugar, almonds, crushed amaretti cookies, and orange marmalade in a separate bowl.

5 Grease a cookie sheet with butter.

6 Lightly flour the counter. Roll out the pasta dough into a thin sheet and cut into 2 inch circles with a plain pastry cutter.

7 Put a spoonful of filling on to each round and then fold in half, pressing the edges to seal. Arrange on the prepared cookie sheet, spacing the ravioli out well.

8 Beat the remaining egg and brush all over the ravioli to glaze. Bake in a preheated oven at 350°F for 20 minutes. Serve hot.

creamy noodle dessert

This rich and satisfying pudding is a traditional Jewish recipe.

Serves 4

4 tbsp butter, plus extra for greasing

6 oz ribbon egg noodles

½ cup cream cheese

1 cup cottage cheese

½ cup superfine sugar

2 eggs, lightly beaten

½ cup sour cream

1 tsp vanilla extract

a pinch of ground cinnamon

1 tsp grated lemon peel

¼ cup slivered almonds

⅜ cup dry white bread crumbs

confectioner's sugar, for dusting

variation

Although not authentic, you could add 3 tbsp raisins with the lemon peel in step 3, if liked.

1 Grease an ovenproof dish with butter.

2 Bring a large pan of water to a boil. Add the noodles and cook until almost tender. Drain and set aside.

3 Beat together the cream cheese, cottage cheese, and superfine sugar in a bowl. Beat in the eggs, a little at a time. Stir in the sour cream, vanilla extract, cinnamon, and lemon peel, and fold in the noodles. Transfer the mixture to the prepared dish and smooth the surface.

4 Melt the butter in a skillet. Add the almonds and cook, stirring constantly, for about 1–1½ minutes, or until lightly colored. Remove the skillet from the heat and stir the bread crumbs into the almonds.

5 Sprinkle the almond and bread crumb mixture over the pudding and bake in a preheated oven at 350°F for 35–40 minutes, or until just set. Dust with a little confectioner's sugar and serve immediately.

3

3

5

raspberry meringues

This simple combination of fudgey meringue topped with yogurt and raspberries is the perfect finale to any meal.

Serves 4

2 large egg whites

1 tsp cornstarch

1 tsp raspberry vinegar

½ cup light muscovado sugar, crushed
    free of lumps

¾ cup low-fat unsweetened yogurt

6 oz raspberries, thawed if frozen

2 tbsp redcurrant jelly

2 tbsp unsweetened orange juice

rose-scented geranium leaves, to decorate

1 Preheat the oven to 300°F. Line a large cookie sheet with baking parchment. In a large, grease-free bowl, whisk the egg whites until very stiff and dry. Fold in the cornstarch and vinegar.

2 Gradually whisk in the sugar, a spoonful at a time, until the mixture is thick and glossy.

3 Divide the mixture into 4 and spoon on to the cookie sheet, spaced well apart. Smooth each into a circle, about 4 inches across, and bake in the oven for 40–45 minutes, or until lightly browned and crisp. Let cool on the sheet.

4 Place the redcurrant jelly and orange juice in a small pan and heat, stirring, until melted. Let cool for 10 minutes.

5 Meanwhile, using a spatula, carefully remove each pavlova from the baking parchment and transfer to a serving plate. Top with unsweetened yogurt and raspberries.

6 Spoon over the redcurrant jelly mixture to glaze. Decorate with the leaves and serve.

variation

Make a large pavlova by forming the meringue into a circle, measuring 7 inches across, on a lined cookie sheet and bake for 1 hour.

1

2

3

marinated peaches

A very simple but incredibly pleasing dessert, which is especially good for a dinner party on a hot summer day.

1

1

cook's tip

There is absolutely no need to use expensive wine in this recipe, so it can be quite economical to make.

cook's tip

The best way to pare the peel thinly from citrus fruits is to use a potato peeler.

Serves 4

4 large ripe peaches

2 tbsp confectioners' sugar, sifted

pared peel and juice of 1 orange

¾ cup medium or sweet white wine, chilled

1 Using a sharp knife, halve the peaches, then remove the pits and discard them. Peel the peaches, if you prefer. Slice the peaches into thin wedges.

2 Place the peach wedges in a glass serving bowl and sprinkle over the sugar.

3 Using a sharp knife, pare the peel from the orange. Cut the orange peel into short, thin sticks, then place them in a bowl of cold water and set aside.

4 Squeeze the juice from the orange and pour over the peaches together with the wine.

5 Let the peaches marinate and chill in the refrigerator for at least 1 hour.

6 Remove the orange peel from the cold water and pat dry with paper towels.

7 Garnish the peaches with the strips of orange peel and serve at once.

3

ricotta & orange desserts

These baked mini-ricotta puddings are delicious served warm or chilled and will keep in the refrigerator for 3–4 days.

1

3

4

Serves 4

1 tbsp butter

½ cup mixed dried fruit

9 oz ricotta cheese

3 egg yolks

¼ cup superfine sugar

1 tsp cinnamon

finely grated peel of 1 orange, plus extra
to decorate

sour cream, to serve

cook's tip

Sour cream has a slightly
sour, nutty taste and is very
thick. It is suitable for
cooking, but has the same fat
content as heavy cream. It can
be made by stirring cultured
buttermilk into heavy cream
and refrigerating overnight.

1 Lightly grease 4 mini pudding basins
or ramekin dishes with the butter.

2 Put the dried fruit in a bowl and
cover with warm water. Let soak for
10 minutes.

3 Beat the ricotta cheese with the egg
yolks in a bowl. Stir in the superfine
sugar, cinnamon, and orange peel, and
mix to combine.

4 Drain the dried fruit in a sieve set
over a bowl. Mix the drained fruit
with the ricotta cheese mixture.

5 Spoon the mixture into the basins or
ramekin dishes.

variation

Use the dried fruit of your
choice for this delicious
recipe.

6 Bake in a preheated oven, at 350°F,
for 15 minutes. The tops should be
firm to the touch, but not brown.

7 Decorate the puddings with grated
orange peel. Serve warm or chilled
with a dollop of sour cream.

baked mascarpone cheesecake

The mascarpone gives this baked cheesecake a wonderfully tangy flavor.

Serves 8

1½ tbsp unsalted butter

5½ oz ginger cookies, crushed

1 oz candied ginger, chopped

1 lb 2 oz mascarpone cheese

finely grated peel and juice of 2 lemons

½ cup superfine sugar

2 large eggs, separated

fruit coulis (see Cook's Tip), to serve

1 Grease and line the base of a 10 inch spring-form cake pan or loose-bottomed pan.

2 Melt the butter in a pan and stir in the crushed cookies and chopped ginger. Use the mixture to line the pan, pressing the mixture about ¼ inch up the sides.

3 Beat together the cheese, lemon peel and juice, sugar, and egg yolks until smooth.

4 Whisk the egg whites until they are stiff and fold into the cheese and lemon mixture.

5 Pour the mixture into the pan and bake in a preheated oven, at 350°F, for 35–45 minutes until just set. Don't worry if it cracks or sinks—this is quite normal.

6 Let the cheesecake stand in the pan to cool. Serve with fruit coulis (see Cook's Tip).

variation

Ricotta cheese can be used instead of the mascarpone to make an equally delicious cheesecake. However, it should be strained before use to remove any lumps.

cook's tip

Fruit coulis can be made by cooking 14 oz fruit, such as blueberries, for 5 minutes with 2 tablespoons of water. Strain the mixture, then stir in 1 tablespoon (or more to taste) of sifted confectioners' sugar. Let cool before serving.

1

2

2

egg mousse with marsala

This well-known dish is really a light but rich egg mousse flavored with Marsala.

Serves 4

5 egg yolks

½ cup superfine sugar

⅓ cup Marsala wine or sweet sherry

amaretti cookies, to serve (optional)

2

2

1 Place the egg yolks in a mixing bowl.

2 Add the sugar to the egg yolks and whisk until the mixture is thick and very pale and has doubled in volume.

3 Place the bowl containing the egg yolk and sugar mixture over a saucepan of simmering water.

4 Add the Marsala wine or sherry to the egg yolk and sugar mixture and continue whisking until the foam mixture becomes warm. This process may take as long as 10 minutes.

5 Pour the mixture, which should be frothy and light, into 4 wine glasses.

6 Serve the zabaglione warm with fresh fruit or amaretti cookies, if you wish.

4

variation

Iced or Semifreddo Zabaglione can be made by following the method here, then continuing to whisk the foam while standing the bowl in cold water. Beat ⅔ cup light cream until it just holds its shape. Fold into the foam and freeze for about 2 hours, or until just frozen.

cook's tip

Any other type of liqueur may be used instead of the Marsala wine or sweet sherry, if you prefer. Serve soft fruits, such as strawberries or raspberries, with the zabaglione—it's a delicious combination!

rich chocolate tiramisu

This is a traditional chocolate dessert from Italy, although at one time it was known as Zuppa Inglese because it was a favorite with the English society living in Florence in the 1800s.

Serves 6

10½ oz dark chocolate

14 oz mascarpone cheese

⅔ cup heavy cream, whipped until it
   just holds its shape

1¾ cups black coffee with
   ¼ cup superfine sugar, cooled

6 tbsp dark rum or brandy

36 lady-fingers, about 14 oz

unsweetened cocoa, to dust

1 Melt the chocolate in a bowl set over a saucepan of simmering water, stirring occasionally. Let the chocolate cool slightly, then stir it into the mascarpone and cream.

2 Mix the coffee and rum together in a bowl. Dip the lady-fingers into the mixture briefly so that they absorb the liquid but do not become soggy.

3 Place 3 lady-fingers on 3 serving plates.

4 Spoon a layer of the mascarpone and chocolate mixture over the lady-fingers.

5 Place 3 more lady-fingers on top of the mascarpone layer. Spread over a layer of mascarpone and chocolate mixture and then place 3 more lady-fingers on top.

6 Let the tiramisu chill in the refrigerator for at least 1 hour. Dust with a little unsweetened cocoa just before serving.

variation

Try adding 1¾ oz toasted, chopped hazelnuts to the chocolate cream mixture in step 1, if you prefer.

cook's tip

Tiramisu can also be served semi-frozen, like ice-cream. Freeze the tiramisu for 2 hours and serve immediately as it defrosts very quickly.

1

1

2

italian apple dessert

This deliciously rich dessert is cooked with cream and apples and is delicately flavored with orange.

Serves 4

1 tbsp butter

2 small eating apples, peeled, cored, and sliced into rings

2¾ oz granulated sugar

2 tbsp white wine

3½ oz bread, sliced with crusts removed (slightly stale French baguette is ideal)

1¼ cups light cream

2 eggs, beaten

pared peel of 1 orange, cut into short, thin sticks

cook's tip

Light cream is the type of cream most commonly used for cooking. However, this type of cream should not be boiled as it will curdle. Also, always add hot liquids to the cream rather than the cream to the liquids, in order to avoid curdling. Light cream has an 18-percent fat content.

variation

For a variation, try adding dried fruit, such as apricots, cherries, or dates, to the pudding, if you prefer.

1 Lightly grease a 2-pint deep ovenproof dish with the butter.

2 Arrange the apple rings in the base of the dish. Sprinkle half of the sugar over the apples.

3 Pour the wine over the apple slices. Add the slices of bread, pushing them down with your hands to flatten them slightly.

4 Mix the cream with the eggs, the remaining sugar, and the orange peel and pour the mixture over the bread. Let soak for 30 minutes.

5 Bake in a preheated oven, at 350°F, for 25 minutes, or until golden and set. Serve warm.

3

3

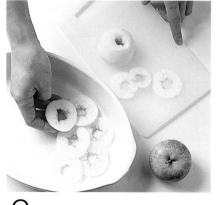

2

citrus salad with almond & honey dressing

Sliced citrus fruits with a delicious almond and honey dressing make an unusual and refreshing dessert.

1

2

5

Serves 4

2 grapefruit, ruby or plain

4 oranges

pared peel and juice of 1 lime

4 tbsp runny honey

2 tbsp warm water

1 sprig of mint, roughly chopped

1 3/4 oz chopped walnuts

1 Using a sharp knife, slice the top and bottom from the grapefruits, then slice away the rest of the skin and pith.

2 Cut carefully between each segment of the grapefruit to remove the fleshy part only.

3 Using a sharp knife, slice the top and bottom from the oranges, then slice away the rest of the skin and pith.

4 Cut between each segment of the oranges to remove the fleshy part. Add to the grapefruit.

5 Place the lime peel, 2 tablespoons of lime juice, the honey, and the warm water in a small bowl. Whisk with a fork to mix the dressing.

6 Pour the dressing over the segmented fruit, then add the chopped mint and mix well. Let chill in the refrigerator for 2 hours for the flavors to mingle.

7 Place the chopped walnuts on a cookie sheet. Lightly toast the walnuts under a preheated medium broiler for 2–3 minutes, or until browned.

8 Sprinkle the toasted walnuts over the fruit and serve.

variation

Instead of the walnuts, you could sprinkle toasted almonds, cashew nuts, hazelnuts, or pecans over the fruit, if you prefer.

summer fruit dessert

A sweet cream cheese dessert that complements the tartness of fresh summer fruits rather well.

Serves 4

1 lb mascarpone cheese

½ cup superfine sugar

4 egg yolks

14 oz frozen summer fruits, such as
    raspberries and redcurrants

redcurrants, to garnish

amaretti cookies, to serve

2

1

2

2 Stir the egg yolks and sugar into the mascarpone cheese, mixing well. Let the mixture chill in the refrigerator for about 1 hour.

3 Spoon a layer of the mascarpone mixture into the bottom of 4 individual serving dishes. Spoon a layer of the summer fruits on top. Repeat the layers in the same order, reserving some of the mascarpone mixture for the top.

4 Let the mousses chill in the refrigerator for about 20 minutes. The fruits should still be slightly frozen.

5 Serve the mascarpone mousses with amaretti cookies.

variation

Try adding 3 tablespoons of your favorite liqueur to the mascarpone cheese mixture in step 1, if you prefer.

1 Place the mascarpone cheese in a large mixing bowl. Using a wooden spoon, beat the mascarpone cheese until smooth.

cook's tip

Mascarpone (sometimes spelled mascherpone) is a soft, creamy cheese from Italy. It is becoming increasingly more available, and you should have no difficulty finding cartons in your local supermarket, or Italian delicatessen.

spiced citrus cake

This is a light and tangy citrus cake better eaten as a dessert than as a cake. It is especially good served after a large meal.

1

2

3

Serves 8

4 eggs, separated

scant ⅔ cup superfine sugar, plus 2 tsp
for the cream

finely grated peel and juice of 2 oranges

finely grated peel and juice of 1 lemon

generous 1 cup ground almonds

2 tbsp self-rising flour

¾ cup light cream

1 tsp cinnamon

¼ cup slivered almonds, toasted

confectioners' sugar, to dust

1 Grease and line the base of a
7 inch round deep cake pan.

2 Blend the egg yolks with the sugar
until the mixture is thick and creamy.
Whisk half of the orange peel and all of
the lemon peel into the egg yolks.

3 Mix the juice from both oranges and
the lemon with the ground almonds
and stir into the egg yolks. The mixture
will become quite runny at this point.
Fold in the flour.

4 Whisk the egg whites until stiff and
gently fold into the egg yolk mixture.

5 Pour the mixture into the pan and
bake in a preheated oven, at 350°F,
for 35–40 minutes, until golden and
springy to the touch. Let cool in the pan
for 10 minutes and then turn out. It is
likely to sink slightly at this stage.

variation

You could serve this cake
with a syrup. Boil the juice
and finely grated peel of
2 oranges, 2¾ oz superfine
sugar, and 2 tbsp of water
for 5-6 minutes until slightly
thickened. Stir in 1 tbsp of
orange liqueur just before
serving.

6 Whip the cream to form soft peaks.
Stir in the remaining orange peel,
cinnamon, and sugar.

7 Once the cake is cold, cover with
the toasted almonds and dust
with confectioners' sugar, then serve
with the cream.

rich vanilla gelato

Italy is synonymous with ice cream. This home-made version of real vanilla ice cream is absolutely delicious and so easy to make.

1

Serves 4-6

2½ cups heavy cream

1 vanilla pod

pared peel of 1 lemon

4 eggs, beaten

2 egg, yolks

6 oz superfine sugar

3

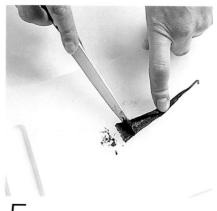

5

cook's tip

To make tutti frutti ice cream, soak 3½ oz mixed dried fruit, such as golden raisins, cherries, apricots, candied peel, and pineapple, in 2 tablespoons of Marsala wine or sweet sherry for 20 minutes. Follow the method for vanilla ice cream, omitting the vanilla pod, and stir in the Marsala or sherry-soaked fruit in step 5, just before freezing.

1 Place the cream in a heavy-based pan and heat gently, whisking. Add the vanilla pod, lemon peel, eggs, and egg yolks and heat until the mixture reaches just below boiling point.

2 Reduce the heat and cook for 8–10 minutes, whisking the mixture continuously, until thickened.

3 Stir the sugar into the cream mixture, then set aside and let cool.

4 Strain the cream mixture through a fine strainer.

5 Slit open the vanilla pod and scoop out the tiny black seeds, then stir them into the cream.

6 Pour the mixture into a shallow freezing container with a lid and freeze overnight until set. Serve when required.

cook's tip

Ice cream is one of the traditional dishes of Italy. Everyone eats it and there are numerous gelato stalls selling a wide variety of flavors, usually in a cone. It is also serve in scoops, and even sliced!

lemon & coffee slushes

A delightful end to a meal or a refreshing way to cleanse the palate between courses, granitas are made from slushy ice rather than frozen solid, so they need to be served very quickly.

Serves 4

LEMON GRANITA

3 lemons

¼ cup lemon juice

½ cup superfine sugar

2¼ cups cold water

COFFEE GRANITA

2 tbsp instant coffee

2 tbsp sugar

2 tbsp hot water

2½ cups cold water

2 tbsp rum or brandy

cook's tip

If you would prefer a non-alcoholic version of the coffee granita, simply omit the rum or brandy and add extra instant coffee instead.

1 To make lemon granita, finely grate the lemon peel. Place the lemon peel, juice, and superfine sugar in a pan. Bring the mixture to a boil and let simmer for 5–6 minutes, or until thick and syrupy. Let cool.

2 Once cooled, stir in the cold water and pour into a shallow freezer container with a lid. Freeze for 4–5 hours, stirring occasionally to break up the ice. Serve as a palate cleanser between dinner courses.

3 To make coffee granita, place the coffee and sugar in a bowl and pour over the hot water, stirring until dissolved.

4 Stir in the cold water together with the rum or brandy.

5 Pour the mixture into a shallow freezer container with a lid. Freeze the granita for at least 6 hours, stirring every 1–2 hours in order to create a grainy texture. Serve with cream after dinner, if you wish.

1

1

2